Social IMC

Social Strategies with Bottom-Line ROI

By:

Randy Hlavac

Lecturer Professor at Northwestern University
Medill Integrated Marketing Communications (IMC) School
CEO of Marketing Synergy, Inc.

D1051302

Media: Social IMC
Social Strategies with Bottom-Line ROI
By Randy Hlavac
Copyright © 2014 by Marketing Synergy, Inc.

ISBN: 1495203662
ISBN-13: 9781495203664
Library of Congress Control Number: 2014900957
CreateSpace Independent Publishing Platform, North Charleston, SC

Printed in the United States of America

10 9 8 7 6 5 4 3 2 1

Published by _____

Website: www.SocialIMC.com

Table of Contents

Foreword

A MANAGERIAL APPROACH TO DIGITAL MEDIA

At the time this Foreword was written, Google listed 2,280,000,000 citations on digital media. (and it took .27 seconds to upload that information). That's why when Randy Hlavac told me he was writing a book on digital media, I thought he was quite mad. How could anyone make sense about a topic that is so ubiquitous, and at the same time, so mysterious to many poor mortals? How could anyone put down on paper, a coherent set of views, principles and practices in a field that seems to reinvent itself about every 20 minutes......new tools, new techniques and yes, even new terminology.

To me, an old fashioned text book writer, who wrote his first book on a Remington Royal manual with a fabric ribbon and a pot of White-Out close by, that sounded like the height of fantasy. Back then, it took me a week just to develop an outline. That's a lifetime in a field where Facebook is only ten years old and Twitter only 6. And, the newest darling, Pinterest with only a few months of marketplace use but millions of users.

I wondered: How could anyone corral the technology, not to mention the managerial challenges of moving from traditional, well developed, well documented media such as print and broadcast, and then, coherently discuss the concepts, approaches and techniques such as you will find in this text.

Yet, Randy persevered. He organized. He synthesized. He framed. And, of course, he edited and honed his view of digital media. A way to think about it. A way to manage it. A way to use it in the dramatically different world of interactivity.

The result? What you are holding in your hand right now. It's the most coherent and usable managerial view of digital media and the digital marketplace available. Randy has done what few other writers have been able to do, capture lightening in bottle (the world of digital media) and give it to us in easy to take doses so that it can be digested and used by any marketing, media or communication manager. Faced with the challenges of making investment decisions which will impact the future of his or her organization, this text provides a clear and guiding light of what must be done, what should be done and most important, given all the technology and tools, can safely be ignored.

The framework Randy uses, that of Engagement, Nurture and then build a Social Media IMC brand will likely be new to many. Given the "here, now and gone" of much digital media, planning and a solid approach to building the brand and the business seems like a foreign tongue. And, in much of the current writing, it is. But, Randy has a different view, a different approach. His notion is that digital media is all about the customer, not the tools and not the technology.

As you will see, Randy builds a strong case for starting with the customer. He argues that the most important element in any digital media discussion, but, often the one that eludes managers is the customer. If I don't know much about customers, it is only natural to fall in love with the latest "bright new shiny new technological innovation". As a result, too often the technique overwhelms the marketer and obscures the view of the customer. Marketers forget that it is not the number of Tweets or Likes that are important, it is the relationship they signify and illustrate among and between customers and brands that really counts.

Throughout the book, Randy keeps coming back to that theme "Start with the customer". Not the media form. Not the product to be promoted. Not with the techno gimmicks that too often dominate the conversation. Always remember, digital media is here for only one reason: to create, build and enhance the relationship between the buyer and seller.

Perhaps the most valuable tool Randy uses in this text is clear, simple, descriptive language. It is digital media for all of us, not the technocrati or the "insiders". It is crafted so that any marketing, communication or brand manager, no matter how well educated at the technical level, can quickly grasp what is happening in the digital media world. Can sort out the grains of knowledge from the bales and bushels of verbiage and discussions which have too long dominated most professional and yes, even the academic literature. Clarity, coherence and communicability. All of that comes through because Randy is a consummate teacher. He wants the reader to learn. He is more interested in that than in pontificating on points and practices.

In short, I'm very pleased that Randy asked me to read his text. I'm even more pleased he asked me to say a few words on behalf of his text at the beginning of your journey into the world of digital media. If you need a guiding light to help you sort through all the mystics of digital media that have been created, you couldn't have a better one than Randy Hlavac.

So, lean back. Listen to what Randy has to say and then put it into practice. As so many have said, digital media is not a destination, it's a journey. And, this is the guidebook you need.

Don E. Schultz
Professor Emeritus in IMC
Northwestern University
March, 2014

Acknowledgments

Professor Emeritus Ted Spiegel was a pioneer in direct marketing. He made the Spiegel catalog one of the finest in the world and was instrumental in the start-up of the Medill Integrated Marketing Communications [IMC] program at Northwestern. Ted was not only responsible for getting me to Northwestern as a Lecturer Professor but continually encouraged me to write this book in Social IMC. Ted made a huge impact on my career and my life.

I also want to thank Professor Emeritus Don Schultz for writing the Foreword to this book, John Lavine, former Dean of the Medill program, and Dan Hoefler. Your guidance and advice were critical to developing this book. I would also like to thank Lecturer Professor Judy Franks and Jeff Davidoff's marketing team for taking time out of their busy schedules to proof read and offer advice on the final book. It really made a difference.

I also want to acknowledge the people who helped me develop these social strategies and who patiently educated me on social and mobile marketing: Steve Dodd, Seth Redmore, Joey Strawn, CK Kerley, Randy Krum, Ellen Valentine, Steffi Decker, Ron Jacobs, Mark Schaefer, Valinda Kennedy & Scott Oliver of IBM and, especially, Jeff Davidoff of ONE.org who both educated me and served as a client and mentor in my Northwestern social marketing classes. I also want to thank our many other clients who helped shape and test these social strategies.

Finally, I also want to thank my family for their support as I developed this book over the last 3 years. Corey my wife, CFO, and editor who suffered through many rewrites of this book, my children Anne, Jeff, and Alicia for their support, and to my mother, father and sisters for their constant encouragement. We finally did it!

1

The Challenge is Clear

You know the challenge. Today, there are literally thousands of studies showing how social and mobile technology are changing the world.[1] While younger demographic cohorts led the transition, social and mobile technologies are now being used by every demographic group[2] and is now an international phenomenon[3]. Whether you are marketing to businesses (B2B) or to consumers (B2C), running a not-for-profit organization, or are a government agency communicating with your constituents, you know the world of social is a vital place you need to be to engage with your high value audiences. With the right social and mobile strategies, your organization can build holistic, database-driven social programs that link your social media to your organization's databases. This means establishing metrics from first social engagement to last engagement with your organization. The key is knowing the successful strategies other organizations are using and matching them to the audiences you want to develop in the future.

While this all sounds great for your organization, most companies have deployed social strategies with no bottom-line metrics. In a 2012 survey from IBM titled "From Stretched to Strengthened: Insights from the Global Chief Marketing Officer Study", the study found most executives are swamped by the rate of change occurring today.[4] When asked about the areas they were least prepared to address, these CMOS cited Big Data, Social Media and the growth of Mobile as their top three threats. Lack of ROI Certainty was one of the top two road-blocks to addressing these challenges.

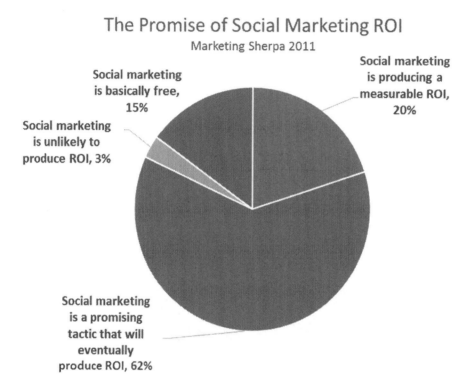

The Promise of Social Marketing ROI

Marketing Sherpa 2011

Social marketing is producing a measurable ROI, 20%

Social marketing is basically free, 15%

Social marketing is unlikely to produce ROI, 3%

Social marketing is a promising tactic that will eventually produce ROI, 62%

The problem with using social in an organization is summarized by a recent survey of CMOs by Marketing Sherpa.[5] They found a strong majority of marketing managers classify social marketing as a promising tactic that may eventually produce ROI, but isn't profitable now. In fact, fully 80% of all of the individuals surveyed could not quantify the return from their social investment.

In this book, we are going to take on the challenge of how to best use social and mobile to achieve your organization's business goals.

We will accomplish this by focusing on the 20% in the survey who do have social and mobile strategies producing bottom-line results. No matter what type of organization you are, we will show you how to develop the best social strategies to achieve your goals.

What Your Business Needs Today

In helping organizations build their social and mobile strategies over the last eight years, we have learned there are four key components you need to incorporate into your social strategy. First, you need social strategies with **bottom-line metrics**. While you may have implemented social programs based on the fact your audiences were moving there, this is not acceptable today. From the Fortune 100 C-level suites to the entrepreneur justifying a start-up to potential investors, you need prove the return on your social and mobile investments. This book will focus on how to measure and cost justify your social programs.

Second, you need a **holistic approach** to social media. While there are pundits who advocate developing site-specific strategies, your audience does not view social this way. They move freely between all types of social media to address their passions and their needs. Today, as Facebook eclipses 1 billion members[6], experts are already warning that teens are now moving away from Facebook and toward new technologies which better meet their needs.[7] Your organization needs a social strategy which accommodates technological change. This book will give you a strategy which remains constant and incorporates change into it when it, inevitably, occurs.

Third, you need a strategy which addresses **Big Data**. A recent IBM study of CEOs identifies this as one of their main concerns in a "Change or Lose" marketplace.[8] This book will show you how to use Big Data to learn about the social habits of your high value audiences in planning your social strategies. It will also demonstrate how to use data to quickly respond when a social visitor is ready to grow their relationship with your organization. By the end of the book, you will be able to see the relationship between Big Data and your social and mobile programs.

Finally, you need a strategy with **_proven results_**. Since 2006, we have been developing social and mobile strategies which have been implemented by organizations throughout the world. We help design, develop and deploy these strategies in businesses, non-profits, news, and governmental organizations. We will highlight best-of-breed examples from the US, Great Britain, South Africa, China and several other countries. Each example was selected to show the strategy and let you see the results these programs are bring to the bottom-line results. You can also find examples from more countries and new cases on our book's website at www.SocialIMC.com. They are categorized by the three social strategies and case type. Like we teach at Northwestern, learning is a lifetime experience and this book will keep you current on the newest examples of organizations deploying social strategies with bottom-line ROI.

Where Do We Start?

In this book, we will explore three different Social strategies. They are Engagement Marketing, Nurture Marketing, and Social IMC. IMC stands for Integrated Marketing Communications and represents a database-driven, 1-to-1 relationship between an organization and an individual. Each strategy builds a different relationship with a target market, and each requires a different level of investment and support from your organization. As you will learn, the key to success is to start with the major audiences you want to develop and select your social and mobile strategies based on the type of relationship you want to establish.

2

Understanding Social Media

In talking with executives throughout the world, there are several characteristics of social which are misunderstood. By clarifying these misconceptions, you will be better able to see the potential of social to grow your organizations and develop strategies which are effective.

1. Social Is Deeper Than You Think

As we studied social strategies, there were many "AH HA" moments. One of the most important came from discussions with Steve Dodd of Boardreader. Boardreader is a major player in social monitoring. They are an organization which deep dives into social media sites to extract the data social monitoring systems use to analyze social chatter.

When we first talked to Steve, he overviewed the types of social media sites from which they extract data. When he discussed bloggers, news sites, and other social media, networking sites like Facebook and Twitter were not among them. When we asked why they were omitted, his response revealed the first misconception we had about social media.

Steve said that Boardreader is after the deep conversations being held in social media. Deep conversations to him meant discussions of significant length and depth to reveal the individual's thoughts and feelings about a topic. While Facebook, Twitter and other social networking sites are big in terms of number of members, the conversations within them are short in content and in duration. While people on social networking sites might be discussing a topic like cancer, the real discussions are on forums, blogs, news and other media. While networks are great at covering trending topics, the deep, long-lasting and significant conversations are deeper within the social cloud.

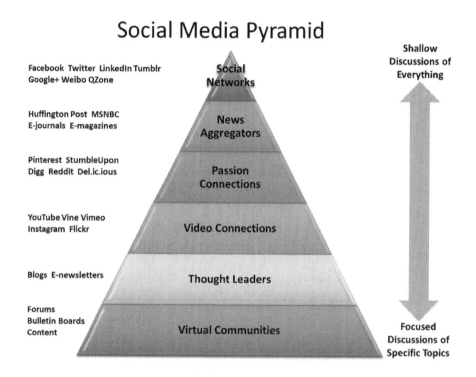

Social Media Pyramid

Facebook Twitter LinkedIn Tumblr Google+ Weibo QZone — **Social Networks**

Huffington Post MSNBC E-journals E-magazines — **News Aggregators**

Pinterest StumbleUpon Digg Reddit Del.ic.ious — **Passion Connections**

YouTube Vine Vimeo Instagram Flickr — **Video Connections**

Blogs E-newsletters — **Thought Leaders**

Forums Bulletin Boards Content — **Virtual Communities**

Shallow Discussions of Everything

Focused Discussions of Specific Topics

Based on our education by Steve and other social experts, we developed this Social Media Pyramid. It is made up of six distinct types of social media sites. They are ranked from top to bottom, not based on the size of the sites, but rather on the nature of the social conversations. At the top, conversations are, for the most part, short and shallow. As we move towards the bottom of the pyramid, the conversations are more long-term and substantial. By better understanding the social pyramid, you will be able to find your high value audiences within the social cloud.

The six levels of the Social Media Pyramid are:

Social Networking Sites: Social networks exist worldwide and let individuals connect with each other and organizations that interest them. These sites are large and consist of individuals of every age, income bracket, and interest. Every conceivable topic is being discussed on social networks. We will use social networking sites to reach our target audiences but, in most of the strategies, we will take them to other social levels to make a more significant engagement with them.

News Aggregator Sites: These are news sites, e-journals, and e-newsletters designed to present text, video, and audio content to their targeted readers. Some of these aggregator sites, like MSNBC or Huffington Post, address a myriad of issues, and serve a diverse readership base. Others have extremely homogeneous, targeted readerships—often just a few or a few hundred people. News aggregator sites are sought out by individuals if they address their interests and passions.

Passion Connection Sites: These sites are designed to allow us to meet with others who support our passions and interests. Sites like Pinterest allow people to meet around topics of their passion. Other sites, like Reddit, allow users to discuss interesting topics and engage with people of a variety of interests. Passion connection sites work if they can make it easy for us to connect with others with similar passions. Unlike a social network on which a discussion of your passions is broadcast to everyone in your network (except for Google+), a discussion on a passion-connection site is more likely to be with others with the exact same interest.

Video Connection Sites: It's amazing to think that today over sixty hours of videos are uploaded to YouTube every minute.[9] From a marketing standpoint, it's important to note that YouTube is now the second largest search site, second only to Google.[10] Why is this important? More and more, your markets are communicating using video rather than text. It fits better into their multi-tasking day, quickly conveys ideas and thoughts, is more engaging, and easily remembered.[11] Today, video sites from YouTube to Vine are changing the way information is being communicated to younger people raised on television and computers.

Thought Leader Sites: The fifth level in the social pyramid consists of bloggers. While business executives are aware of blogs, many don't realize how big, influential, and pervasive they are. Today, there are over 18.7 million blogs in existence on every conceivable topic. The largest blog has over forty-six million unique visitors each month, and 77 percent of all Internet users read blogs each month.[12] Your organization's social marketing strategy needs to incorporate bloggers and blog articles to effectively reach and engage any target market. One influential blogger may be talking to a sizable percentage of a high value market you are seeking. Using them, and generating your own blog content are great ways to cut through the clutter and go directly to the target markets you want to impact.

Virtual Community Sites: This is the largest and least understood part of social media. Every day, virtual communities are being formed by engaged individuals who want to address an issue confronting them or a passion they have. These communities become a horizontal discussion among individuals with similar interests, as they attempt to address the challenges they're confronting.[13] Virtual communities are very different from social networks because they're extremely focused. Virtual communities can range from a few members to millions, and are formed to address both business and personal needs and passions. While individual communities may be small, groups of them—all focused on the same issue or need— become massive collections of homogeneous individuals. If they're your target market, virtual communities become an effective way to connect.

In developing our social strategies, we will treat these levels holistically. If your target audience uses a social level, you will want to engage them there. As we build the three social strategies, we will use social monitoring and our knowledge of social developed in this chapter, to determine the best way to engage, empower and acquire your high value audiences.

2. Social Networks and Virtual Communities Behave Differently

As we develop our social marketing strategies, the value of private virtual communities will become clearer. They are the places where deep discussions are occurring among people who are talking about the challenges your products and services address. One of the keys to success is to become a part of these virtual communities in a way that benefits them and your organization.

Characteristics	Social Networks	Virtual Communities
Goals	Linkage & Conversation	Accomplishing its Mission
Creators	Entrepreneur	Individuals
Nature of the Conversation	Shallow & Broad	Focused & Deep
Size and Number	Big and Few	Smaller but Many
Registration	Used for Connection	Used for Control
Management	Company	Members

Social networking sites are created by entrepreneurs to allow people to connect with each other. To use them, you need to go through a registration process in which you establish log-in information and a profile other users can find to connect with you. The goal of these sites is to allow you to link with friends, relatives, and businesses. Once on the site, you can begin discussing any topic, passion, or area of interest. At any point in time, there are conversations about every conceivable topic (and many you can't conceive of). The conversation tends be relatively shallow and quick.

Virtual communities are at the opposite end of the social spectrum. They're formed by individuals to address a key topic or area of great importance to them. While they have a registration process like social networks, they're used for very different reasons. While a few virtual communities are public, most allow you to view their site but you must register to participate in it. These are called private virtual communities.

In a private virtual community, your registration information is used for three purposes. First, because the virtual community consists of people addressing their needs, they want to ensure that new members are also dedicated to their community mission. For many exclusive sites, admission occurs only after you pass the vetting process.

Second, virtual communities are managed by members, and the registration process is important to this function. In a later chapter, we will examine virtual sites where members can black ball other members who are not positively contributing to the site, and promote others whose information is useful in achieving the community mission. Finally, virtual communities use detailed registration information to determine the interests of their users to create content of high relevance to them. Unlike social networking sites, virtual communities are formed to help people address their passions and needs. If they become irrelevant, the virtual community will shrink and vanish. Knowing their member's needs is critical to the community's success.

The most important difference is that private virtual communities are on a very specific mission and are not there to discuss every possible topic. Go to Circle of Moms (http://www.circleofmoms.com/) and you can see mothers and family experts addressing every stage in the raising of children and creating a strong family. Want to discuss restoring Plymouth Roadrunner muscle cars from the 1960s? Try the Plymouth Roadrunner Forum (http://www.69roadrunner.net/mopar/forum.php). There are thousands and thousands of virtual community sites on every conceivable topic, and each is dedicated to a specific mission. Right now, there are virtual communities discussing issues and topics related to your organization. In your social marketing strategy, you need to find them in order to link up with prospects and customers actively discussing the subjects that are important to your organization. Find these communities and you can link to huge percentages of your high-value target markets. They're out there and talking in detail and can be accessed if you know how to find and approach them.

3. Virtual Communities Form For Different Reasons

In traditional marketing channels, we tend to segment based on the demographic and lifestyle characteristics of the businesses or individuals. While your high value audiences in social also have these same types of descriptive characteristics, they are less important in building your social strategy. This is because virtual communities and other user controlled social sites develop for reasons beyond their demographic characteristics.

For your organization to find and engage with private virtual communities, you need to understand why they form. It could be something innately important to the individual—what we call a passion—or it can be to address an event created by some external force—which we call a *trigger event*. External forces could be a life stage or some event happening in your personal life or a planned or unplanned event at work that impacts your professional life.

The Passion Community

Passion communities are formed because people are driven to engage with others about things important to them. There are passion communities focused on raising kids, fashion trends, politics of all types, sports teams, and every other topic you can think of. As individuals, we have feelings about many things, and if it resonates with us, we have the potential to seek a passion community to discuss our interests.

While passion communities may not seem to apply to business professionals, nothing could be further from the truth. There are business passion communities where CEOs talk management, CMOs talk marketing, or internal auditors discuss their craft. There are engineering and programming sites where passionate professionals discuss and improve their skills. Regardless of the industry or the job, there are passion communities where business professionals network and engage.

In building our marketing strategies to engage passion markets, it's important to note that they're always seeking the new and the current. As Heidi Klum says, "One day you're in, the next day you're out."[14] When we develop a social site to engage with any passion market, the focus will be on trendy, up-to-date, and relevant information. In the second part of the book, we will consider using gamification and other engagement devices to make the social site a place where members can express and explore their passions with others.[15]

When you build a passion community support site, you will need to continually create new events and add new information to keep the passionate members engaged. For example, if you are using webinars with experts central to the community's interests, you will need to host them several times each year to keep the passionate members talking and coming back. You will also need to be on the lookout for new experts to keep the conversation lively. For passion communities, the focus is on new and different.

The Trigger Event Community

Trigger Event Communities are very different. This type of community forms because there is an external need to engage with others. In our personal lives, we have trigger events every time we move to a new life stage or something happens in our personal or family lives. Having a baby, getting married, graduating from college, becoming ill, getting a new car, retiring, and millions more events, will move us to seek expertise and engagement using social media.

Businesses, too, have trigger events that create communities. Business changes and new technologies often move business professionals to seek out their peers on social media. Once the trigger event happens, or is about to happen, and we know we need to learn more about how to handle it, many of us will attempt to find answers through social engagement.

Strategically, trigger-event communities have very different social structures. In a trigger event community, members seek out experts who have traveled the road they are about to travel. They want content to educate them on how best to travel it. For trigger event communities, the focus is on proven and reliable, not on the new and trendy. Everyone in a trigger event community is on a journey, and your goal should be twofold. First, identify where they are in their journey. Second, use your trigger event community site to get them the information they need to accomplish it. Your goal should be to help them move from where they are today to the destination they want to reach. If your site helps them on their journey, they will keep coming back.

When teaching community identification at Northwestern, we stress to the graduate students that passion communities contain permanent members who are always seeking insider insights and updated information. Give them an edge and they will keep coming back. Trigger-event communities are permanent sites with temporary members. The member thinks, "Help me address my needs as I move through the trigger event, and I will stay with you until the event is handled." However, as one travels the trigger-event journey, others are joining every day to start on their journeys. Help them along the way, and you will have an effective site.

Regardless of the type of community you're engaging, your best role is to be a trusted expert within the community. To accomplish this goal, you need to provide content, information, and guidance highly relevant to the community. Give the members tools and information to help them accomplish their mission and they'll seek you out in the social conversation.

3

The Engagement Marketing Strategy

As we learned earlier, Marketing Sherpa discovered that 80 percent of all companies deploy social strategies with no bottom-line ROI. Engagement marketing is the strategy they're using. Most companies develop their social strategies as a way to distribute content designed to engage with the visitors to their social networking sites—particularly Facebook. They develop content, place it on their site, and then tell their target markets about it using traditional and social marketing. Visitors who are attracted to the site are asked to do two things. First, they're asked to like or friend the site. This allows them to receive more communications in the future. The second is to tell their friends about it. This gets the content to the exact people the organization is trying to target. If this works really well, we say the content went viral.

One of the strengths of Engagement Marketing is the breadth of its applications for business and consumer marketers. At its most sophisticated, Engagement Marketing can be used to reach millions of people and significantly grow the social footprint of an organization. At the opposite end, it can be used to distribute coupons and sales information effectively. Because it is relatively easy to develop, straight-forward to deploy, requires little action from your visitors, and can impact your target markets, many companies use Engagement Marketing as their primary social strategy. However, as we'll see as we examine all three strategies, Engagement Marketing develops the weakest relationship with your high value markets.

Developing and Deploying an Engagement Marketing Strategy

Engagement Marketing is designed to develop an anonymous relationship with your social visitors. While you know their network name (or handle), engaging with your organization does not require them to give personal data to build a knowledge base about them. As a result, when they make a purchase from your organization, you cannot directly match their purchase back to your social programs. You know

who they are when they purchase, but there is no way to link their purchase back to their social network name. While there are some ways to, at least, develop an understanding of their purchase behaviors, the nature of the Engagement Marketing relationship is anonymous between the organization and its social visitors.

To design, develop and deploy an effective Engagement Marketing strategy, there are five steps you need to take. The Integrated Marketing Communications (IMC) business model always starts with a target market. Today, people want you to engage them directly. To accomplish that, you need to define a target market, develop insights into their defining characteristics, and then build your marketing strategy around their needs, wants, and aspirations. For all three social strategies, we will start with identifying a high value market you want to better develop and then build the strategy toward them.

Target Broadly

One of the defining characteristics of Engagement Marketing is that it develops an anonymous relationship with its target markets. That doesn't mean the target market is unimportant. It's the exact opposite. In order to create the type of content that works well in an

Engagement Marketing strategy, you need to deeply understand and develop content specifically for a desired target market. However, because you will not be engaging them in a one-to-one conversation, you can be broader in your targeting than with the other two social strategies.

The first step in building an Engagement Marketing strategy is to define potential high-value markets you want to develop. Because the goal of Engagement Marketing is to get the largest social footprint possible, you ideally want to identify a broad target market for your Engagement Marketing efforts. Next, you will want to establish both the size and, if possible, potential value of each market. By defining and quantifying your target markets, you will be positioned to develop the content which will most likely go viral and drive your audience to your social sites.

To accomplish this, you will probably need data to best define your current and desired target audiences. For consumer markets, demographic and attitudinal data can be obtained from data provider companies like Acxiom, Experian, and InfoUSA. For businesses, companies like Dunn and Bradstreet can provide you information on the business and the individual on your database systems. They can tell you the individual's title, as well as information on the size, type, and SIC codes of the business, whether an individual has a home or satellite office, and much more.

You can analyze this descriptive data combined with the purchasing information on your database to break your organization's markets into unique segments. Analyzing the demographic, attitudinal, and purchase (behavioral) attributes of each unique segment will allow you to develop a persona of the average individual within each segment. If you are targeting segments that exist on your database, knowing their purchase tendencies and their value to your organization gives you a way to balance your investment against possible returns. Are you a start-up? There are local, regional, national, and international panels you can use to develop the same insights.

The next step is to quantify them. Once you have your markets defined, use secondary sources to further refine and quantify them. For nearly any business or consumer markets, there are relatively up-to-date business and financial analyses that you can access—often for free—through the Internet. Many of these analyses can provide you with additional insights about your potential target markets, and many of them size and place a value on each market segment. You can find secondary research from companies like Forrester and IBM, and publications that track consumer and business markets.

If you have trouble quantifying your markets, you can also look at online database systems like those of InfoUSA (www.infousa.com). These online databases let you enter the demographic and attitudinal descriptions of your business or consumer target markets and will return a count of the number of individuals or households/businesses meeting those criteria. You can also order e-mail, telephone, or direct mail lists of these individuals from these organization. If you are targeting a local, regional, or national (US or Canada) market, online databases can help you determine the size of these markets.

One more step you may want to do in quantifying your target markets: if you know the value of the first purchase of each unique segment, multiply their first purchase revenue with the total size of the market segment, and you can determine their potential value. Even though the Engagement Marketing strategy can't directly measure sales resulting from the program, it often provides insight into the total value each market has for your organization. It might help you prioritize the markets you want to invest in with your Engagement Marketing program.

Once you have defined and quantified the audiences you want to develop, you now have the numbers and insights you need to begin developing your content. In Engagement Marketing, the larger your initial target audience, the more impact you will likely have in the social marketplace.

Create Awesome Content

Powerful content is the key to developing an Engagement Marketing strategy. You want to develop content so engaging, so unexpected, and so powerful, that your target markets will be compelled to take action and tell their friends about it. When this occurs, your Engagement Marketing strategy allows you to initially reach a relatively small percentage of the total target market who will then do the rest. As we teach, one awesome content and one actively engaged target individual will produce hundreds if not thousands of viral communications as each layer tells their friends, who then tell their friends. This works in both business and consumer markets.

So what makes something Awesome? Remember, awesome is in the eyes of your target market. For some markets, awesome might be a series of really great videos that are funny, engaging, and so great that people must tell their friends about them. For other markets, it might be a coupon or special deal. For others, it might be an infographic or other type of visual content. It really depends on your target market and what they find attractive.

While Awesome is in the eyes of each target market, there is a content development model you should consider. I was recently talking to Steffi Decker, of Chong + Koster. Steffi is a resource we use in our graduate program to discuss Facebook advertising and other social media. I asked Steffi how she would define Awesome content, and she said she liked the definition used by Upworthy, a social site created by Chris Hughes, a cofounder of Facebook. They define Upworthy content as content being at an intersection of awesome, relevant, and visual. While this definition works for Upworthy, we broadened it to be more relevant to companies targeting either businesses or consumers.

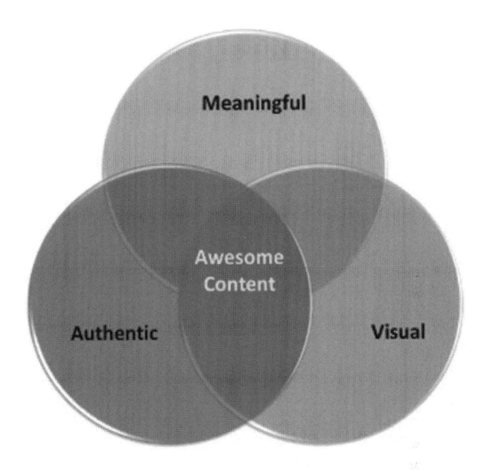

While we will use a slightly modified model, you can find the original Upworthy design on this blog article by the organization. Upworthy is a good source of awesome content being developed by companies throughout the world.[16]

There are three dimensions you need to consider in developing Awesome content. First, Awesome content must be meaningful to the members of the target audience. If it's not something that interests them, there will be no engagement and no viral activity. They will simply ignore it.

So how do you ensure it's meaningful to them? As you develop content ideas, you might want to discuss it with a few members of your target market. Show them the concepts and ask them to rate it for you. Another way is to show it to some of the influential bloggers who are talking to your desired target market. If these groups find it really engaging and interesting, it has taken the first step toward being awesome.

A second important dimension is it must be Authentic. By Authentic we mean the content you're developing must be, in some way, related to the expertise and brand positioning of your organization. It must be an overlap of your organization's expertise with the interests of the target market. While you want your Awesome content to go viral, it's more than just doing something controversial or outside what people know your organization is about.

The final dimension is that it should be visual; however, visual does not mean a video. It must be something that attracts the eye of the target market and draws them to the content. In the next chapter, we'll look at Engagement Marketing programs that use video, streamed webinars, and Pinterest postings at the center of their Engagement Strategy for different target markets. The key is your content should be visual to best appeal to your target market. Infographics are a good source for visual content.

In my graduate social marketing classes at Northwestern, we ask Randy Krum—an expert on Infographics—to discuss how they're developed and their effectiveness as Awesome content in Engagement Marketing. Randy's blog, titled Cool Infographics (http://www.coolinfographics.com/), presents some of the best Infographics developed for business and consumer marketing, and his organization—Infonewt—works with businesses and governmental agencies on how to use infographics to tell a compelling story. In his discussions with us, Randy shows how an effectively developed infographic can go viral in a target market for a long period of time—often years—and can have a major impact on an organization's SEO (search engine optimization) for key search terms.

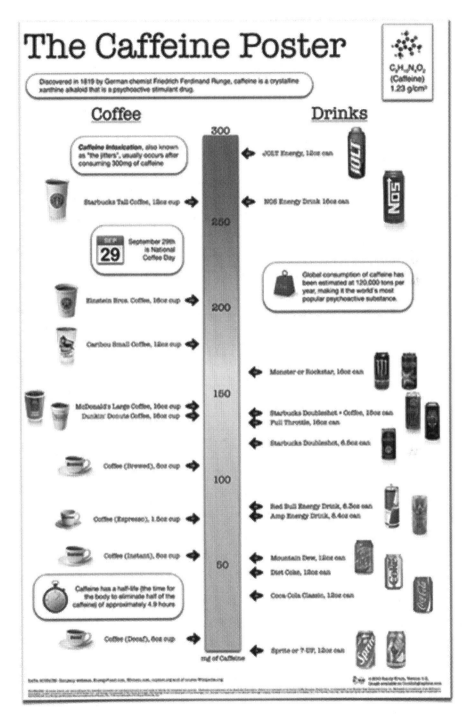

Done effectively, an infographic will be picked up by bloggers, other websites, and creators of other media to virally impact your desired target markets. Randy relates that one of the keys to success is to tell your target audience something they really want to know. Don't sell your products or services, but give them knowledge about a topic of interest to them.

Create and Execute a Go Social Marketing Program

At this point in the process, you have created Awesome content designed to appeal to a specific target market or markets. It's designed to get them excited about your site and has links that allow them to Friend your social networking site and tell their friends and followers  about your new content. However, right now they have no idea that your content exists or—perhaps—even that your organization exists. You need to change that by creating a Go Social marketing program.

In building your Go Social program, there are two critical things to remember. First, you only have a short time to get the attention of your target market(s). They love content they think is really awesome, but only for a short period of time. After a while, they move on to the next Awesome content from someone else. So you will need to strike quickly, get them excited, and then let them do their viral thing.

Second, remember they're on all parts of the social pyramid. This means you need to develop a program that goes where they are. If you create Awesome print content like an infographic, consider developing a short thirty-second to one-minute video showing and discussing it. Place it on your YouTube channel with search terms designed to attract your target market, and end the video with the bitly link to your content. Keep in mind that YouTube is the second biggest search site, and if your target market is using it to find Awesome things, you need to be there too.[17]

Before you create your Go Social plan, take some time to review what you know about your target market and their social tendencies. Where are they in the social pyramid? What are the virtual communities they use to discuss topics related to you? Who are the influential bloggers and key experts who are important to you? What are the hash tags they're using to link up on Twitter? What are the print and electronic media they like to get information related to you? All of these channels will be used in your program so take some time to prepare a list of sources you will want to develop in your Go Social marketing plan.

Next, establish a launch date, and create a series of short sales messages you can use on Facebook, Twitter, and the other social networking sites used by your target market. Remember, you only have a short time to reach to your target markets and move them to action. A focused effort is important. However, to do it effectively, you need to vary the message to find the best way to impact your target market and move them to action.

To create and test effective messages, we recommend developing a messaging schedule spreadsheet. For your Facebook page, create a graphic and message that you can release once every week. Because Facebook is likely a key page in your Engagement Marketing strategy, you need to have resources to monitor it daily. You don't necessarily have to monitor it in real time, but you need to be aware of responses to your offering or the link to your offering. We like to use HootSuite to track multiple social sites and the responses our offerings are creating.

For Twitter, consider one or more messages every day about your Awesome content. You can use the same message and repeat it using the hash tags your markets use to discuss relevant topics. You can also vary the message and test what works best. If your target markets use Pinterest or other Passion sites, you need to be there too. In developing your personas, if your target market members are going to community sites to get information, you need to be there too. For example, if you're targeting mothers, community sites like Circle of Moms (http://www.circleofmoms.com/) are great sites to find them. There are virtual communities for every target market. You just need to find them and then let them know about your Awesome content.

Entertain Them

If your Engagement Marketing program is going after a large market, members of that market will often begin discussing it on Twitter, Facebook, and other social networking pages. As you launch your social programs, you need to monitor all these social channels

to read and, where possible, respond to their comments and questions—in real time if possible. They are taking the time to engage with you and will be disappointed—and often bitter—if you don't respond to their comments. Keep the conversation as focused on their comments as possible, and avoid selling your products and services. Your goal is to make it a fun and interesting engagement so they will be open to future content tailored to them. Avoid the temptation to sell your products and services. That will stop the engagement immediately.

Regardless of the size of your Engagement Marketing program, keep in mind that social is an engaging, real-time media. You must allocate staff time to monitor your social networking sites to respond to the comments and questions from your new visitors. They want to engage with you, so you must take the time and make the effort to solidify the social relationship. Remember, they are on your site to have fun and engage with you about your Awesome content. Make it a positive experience for them.

Strengthen the Relationship

In addition to engaging with your new social friends, your strategy should also include new content designed to maintain the new relationship. For some companies, it means developing new content designed to allow the target market to maintain the buzz and keep the viral activity going.

Other companies attempt to build on their new relationships by offering sales specials or coupons to purchase their products and services. They offer the types of products most likely to be purchased by their target market to keep the relationship relevant. Others offer new content designed to begin moving their new friends toward a purchase.

Whether you want to continue to build the relationship or try to move them toward purchasing your products and services is highly dependent on the types of products you sell and the complexity of the sales relationship. Whether it's a product, sales offer, or more great creative material, you need to build into your plan what you will do when a successful first effort occurs. You have new visitors to your social site who will be attentive for a short time to new content you post. Be sure your Engagement Marketing plan is ready to capitalize on your success. Relationships must be built quickly in social, and like traditional marketing, the relationship is solidified with the second social activity. Plan for this second relationship effort, and have it ready when your first content goes viral.

Engagement Marketing Results Metrics

In the Engagement Marketing strategy, effectiveness is primarily measured using the social metrics, so it makes sense to start there. Every social networking system has a way to measure the strength of your social site. On Facebook, it's the number of Likes. On Twitter and Pinterest, it's the number of followers. On LinkedIn, it's the number of connections. Because these metrics are easy to access, simple to use, and consistent over time, they're the primary metrics for the Engagement Marketing Strategy.

When companies are considering deploying an Engagement Marketing Strategy, they establish specific growth goals for the social networks they will include in the program. Several CMOs I work with have Engagement Marketing programs, and all have very specific social growth targets. The most common among bigger companies is a goal statement like, "We want this program to allow us to reach one million "Likes" on Facebook by the end of the year." Or it might be, "We are targeting a 200 percent growth in our social site at an acquisition cost of less than seventy-five cents per new Friend." These numeric goals can be established for any of the social media and they use likes, followers, and other measures to track the number of individuals you're attracting to your organization pages.

What about sales? As defined in this chapter, Engagement Marketing is designed to develop an anonymous relationship. This means we cannot directly link engagement activities to final sales. While this strategy does not link individuals to product purchases, there are ways marketers can develop insights into the effectiveness of the Engagement Marketing efforts.

A recent study by the Altimeter Group identified three primary research methodologies CMOs use to measure the sales impact of their Engagement Marketing programs. These are:

- Anecdotal: Talking to new customers about the role social played in their sales decision.

- Correlation: Examining sales data to see if there is an impact on the number of items purchased or total dollars for social and non-social users.
- Multivariate: Comparing two data sets over time—one exposed to social and the other not – to see if there is a statistically significant difference.

All three of these produce metrics that CMOs can use to justify their Engagement Marketing investment; however, it's important to emphasize all of these are post-purchase and actually produce a hard link between your Engagement Marketing program and purchases of your products and services. To really know if an individual who first came to your site via social media became a customer, you need a database linking their social activities to your sales and marketing systems. This is the strength of the other two strategies discussed in this book.

Strategy Limitations

If your organization is considering developing and deploying any type of Engagement Marketing strategy, what are the limitations you need to consider? First, remember that the focal point of an Engagement Marketing strategy is the social network. Most of these strategies rely heavily on engagement using Facebook, Twitter, LinkedIn, Google+, or similar social networking systems used in other countries. The data and relationship information on these systems is controlled by the system owner and is rarely provided to the organization maintaining an organization page or pages on these systems.

As a result of the lack of data on the individual, relationships developed using the Engagement Marketing strategy are anonymous. If we decide to shoot a video responding to a tweet made by @Tiffany94, we can message her through Twitter and refer to her in the video, but we don't really know if @Tiffany94 is named Tiffany, is a woman, or the meaning of 94. While, as we'll discuss in the next section, knowing the individual on a one-on-one basis is not necessary for every type of marketing program, it's a major limitation with the Engagement Marketing strategy. It's designed to attract and engage a large market and attract them to your social networking site.

In addition to anonymous relationships, most of the engagement is one way. Engagement Marketing programs are designed to attract thousands if not hundreds of thousands of individuals to your social networking site. While your team can talk to individuals and some major corporations like McDonalds have many individuals who engage with their visitors for key Engagement programs, most companies do not have the resources or the time to engage with everyone. In fact, if you're growing your social site from a hundred thousand to a million Likes, which one of our example companies did, then your one-to-one interactions are with a small minority of your social base. For the most part, Engagement Marketing is a one-way engagement in which you provide awesome content, and the social target markets respond by telling others about your content and Liking your page (or following you).

Because Engagement Marketing must engage with most of the people you're engaging through your social networks, a big limitation is that it must deliver a broad brand message. In other words, most really successful Engagement Marketing programs are designed for a broad, diverse, comingled market with different product expectations. As a result, you'll note that most Engagement Marketing programs do not cite specific brand messages that might alienate specific target markets. They tend to position the organization and its products with a broad brand message and not tailor it to a specific target market. Broad is better.

Finally, Engagement Marketing does not produce a direct linkage to your organization and its sales and marketing operations. Its metrics are generally social networking based. They focus on growing the organization's social footprint. As a result, Engagement Marketing programs do not produce a marketing database of an individual's information, nor can they take advantage of who the individual is and what their relationship is with your organization. Unlike the other two strategies we'll examine, those links don't exist in an Engagement Marketing program.

Best Applications

From the preceding paragraphs you might get the impression there are few situations where an organization should employ an Engagement Marketing social strategy. Nothing is further from the truth. In fact, I recommend most companies use Engagement Marketing for the majority of their markets.

Remember the 80–20 rule? Most of your customers and prospects are not your highest value markets. They are the 80 percent who produce 20 percent of your total revenue. These are the market segments most appropriate for an Engagement Marketing strategy. These less productive markets will benefit from your engaging them through social networking sites and will engage if you give them awesome content they can use. For them, the anonymous relationship is not a hindrance, and they will return if you offer coupons, information, and other content that interests them.

The Engagement Marketing strategy is ideal for packaged goods companies or companies that can offer their products without a deep knowledge of the individual. If your product is an impulse, requires little sales development, and can be purchased online or at a retail location, Engagement Marketing is probably your best social strategy.

Engagement Marketing is also great for customer service interactions and new product introductions. As customers comment, deployment of focused content may not only answer their questions or concerns, but often engages many individuals. New product introductions—especially if the product's target markets are broad—are great using an Engagement Marketing strategy.

Engagement Marketing Summary

Engagement Marketing is a great strategy if your goal is to maximize your social footprint. Why do that? If you're using Facebook to distribute coupons, announce sales, or promote new products, this strategy is great. In each of these instances, you really don't need to know each individual on your social site, but you want large numbers to engage them.

One of the advantages of Engagement Marketing is its scalability. Engagement Marketing is a strategy that can effectively engage a large target market with an awesome set of content. You can deploy the content across multiple media (text, video, and audio) and across the spectrum of social levels where your market resides. It's a great way to impact markets to announce or position goods and services that are likely to be impulse purchases requiring few steps from engagement to purchase.

Engagement Marketing programs can also be used by small business. Awesome content could be a webinar on a really important topic to your target audience, special announcements or coupon offers designed for a specific market segment, or some other lower cost content offering. The key is to invest in a marketing campaign that reaches your target market using the channels appropriate for the market. If you're a brick and mortar operation, you can use QR codes in your stores, e-mail to your customers, and your social pages to best reach and engage your markets. For new product announcement, special sales, coupons, and other engagement opportunities, Engagement Marketing might be the best social strategy, especially if the value of the market is relatively low.

Engagement Marketing
Target Broadly
Create Awesome
Go Social
Entertain
Strengthen

To review, the Engagement Marketing strategy is developed and deployed using a five step methodology. You start with a market you highly value or want to develop because of its potential to your organization. You then create awesome content designed to thrill and engage your market. Once created, you need to develop a Go Social plan that uses traditional and social media to develop buzz within your target market about your awesome content. Done correctly, they'll join your social networking site and then they'll tell their friends and followers about it. If it's truly awesome in their eyes, their friends and followers will tell *their* friends and followers, and it will go viral.

As the program deploys, you'll want to monitor your social media sites and engage with your new friends. You can do this spontaneously, or you can have planned messages to engage with them. It will keep them engaged with you and will begin to strengthen the experience. After a period of time, you need to roll out new content or offers to strengthen the relationship even more. The more you can engage them in your social world, the more they'll remember and respond to your organization and your offers.

Characteristic	Engagement Marketing
Goals	Social footprint
Relationship	Anonymous
Content	Awesome
Marketing	Viral
Metrics	Social

In summary, the Engagement Marketing strategy is powerful and very scalable. The main limitation is that it's an anonymous relationship. If your organization wants to build its social footprint, especially in lower value or marginal markets, engagement marketing is a great strategy to use. In addition, if your products and service are more of an impulse purchase, then an Engagement Marketing strategy designed to make the market aware of your products is an effective investment for your firm. While you sacrifice trackability and linkage to your sales and marketing systems, sometimes it's unnecessary, and in those cases, Engagement Marketing is an effective strategy to use.

4

Engagement Marketing Case Studies

The case study chapters are designed to use videos and images to show you the components and results from each case example. While we have included links in this book, occasionally YouTube, Vimeo and other links will fail. If you cannot get them to open, you can find working copies, as well as newer case examples, on the book's website at www.SocialIMC.com.

In this chapter, we'll explore a variety of Engagement Marketing strategies at work. Some of the examples, like Old Spice, required a major investment in the social marketplace. Others, like Honda and Cadbury, were lower-investment programs. However, each is an example of how to develop and deploy an Engagement Marketing strategy.

The one type of program we did not include an example of is an extremely low-cost program. Near my home is an excellent deli. They use Engagement Marketing to grow their social footprint by offering coupons, sale items and promotions for new deli items. In their deli, their napkin holders have QR codes that allow visitors to easily Like them on Facebook in order to become a part of their community. As they added the ability to ship orders worldwide, they grew their social footprint by offering special items, and advertised on Facebook and other media developed for the international markets. Today, their Engagement Marketing program is successful in engaging with their deli fans throughout the world. It keeps them linked to their customers and prospects and is an integral part of their marketing efforts.

In this section, we will explore three very different applications of the Engagement Marketing Strategy. They are Cadbury Dairy Milk "Thumbs Up" and Old Spice's "Manly Man".

Note: All of the examples in this chapter have been developed from YouTube and Vimeo videos produced by the organization or their advertising agencies. Analysis was also developed from examination of articles featuring organization executives or advertising managers on the campaigns used here.

Old Spice "The Man Your Man Could Smell Like"

When it comes to highly successful Engagement Marketing programs, one organization immediately comes to mind—Old Spice. Their Engagement Marketing strategy shows how you can use multimedia to deploy multiple examples of Awesome content to engage with a high value target market. While many of you will recognize some of the television advertisements, Old Spice's "Manly Man" is much more than just a series of advertising commercials.

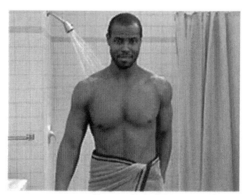

Old Spice – The Man your Man could Smell Like campaign
Uploaded Feb 2010 link http://youtu.be/owGykVbfgUE

In 2010, Old Spice gave their ad agency, Weiden+Kennedy, a unique marketing challenge. The organization was introducing a new men's product—body wash. It was a real challenge. Not only was the marketplace crowded with competitors, but most had established positions in the marketplace. What Weiden+Kennedy needed was a unique, awesome approach to really impact their target market.

In addition to a social effort, the organization would also distribute coupons and have specials to help drive respondents to stores or to online merchants. By combining the social effort with traditional couponing and special sales efforts, the organization wanted to not only engage with the market but move them to action. Their social program got the attention of the target market, and the in-store, online, and traditional coupon distribution systems would aid in moving from engagement to purchase.

Target Broadly

In introducing its new line of male body products, Old Spice made a significant decision. Rather than target the man, they decided to build an Engagement Marketing program designed to appeal to young wives and girlfriends. These individuals either make the decision to purchase products for their men or significantly influence the decision. Their goal was to create an Engagement Marketing program that would directly appeal to their aspirations and goals, and indirectly, position Old Spice products as a way for their man to have that manly scent. Notice that in their Engagement Program, they did not ask the individual to take any action related to purchasing Old Spice products. They just made it fun for the woman to consider a life with a better-smelling man and positioned Old Spice as a way to help achieve this goal.

Create Awesome

Weiden+Kennedy wanted to really impact and engage a unique segment of the market. They wanted to make men's body products interesting, fun to discuss and, most importantly, fun to tell others about. They wanted it to go viral. Because their target markets were young and heavy users of social, it made sense to use social to deliver awesome content and measure its impact. Engagement Marketing was the strategy, and they wanted millions of friends on Facebook, Twitter and other media to show the growth.

Old Spice – The Man your Man could Smell Like campaign
Uploaded Feb 2010 link http://youtu.be/owGykVbfgUE

The social campaigns created by Weiden+Kennedy were truly Awesome. They hired Isaiah Mustafa to personify the manly man who uses Old Spice products. The organization then created a multimedia campaign to create buzz about the new product.

The Engagement Marketing strategy focused on Facebook, YouTube, and Vimeo to broadcast a series of videos designed to engage the women and have fun with the product. This is one of their best ones, titled "The man your man could smell like" (http://youtu.be/owGykVbfgUE). It was the first in a series of commercials that introduced their new body wash to the target market.

When you look at the commercial, you can see it has all of the components that make it awesome to the target market. It's visual, relevant, and meaningful. It also appeals to the aspirations of women who want their man to smell better.

While you probably remember the advertisements from television, Weiden+Kennedy first released them on YouTube and Vimeo to create a viral buzz in their target market. Supported by their Go Social marketing program, the video and the concept went viral before the advertisements were run on cable television to reach a large target market. The viral activity made the program huge in a matter of days.

Go Social

To promote the awesome concept, Weiden+Kennedy used Facebook and Twitter advertising to start and, later, maintain the buzz. By placing the video on YouTube and Vimeo, they also attracted the people who search these sites. Social was a key way to build awareness and ramp the buzz about the product and their viral video.

In addition to the social components, the organization also used traditional cable television and print advertising in periodicals, including newspapers, to reach their target markets. They also supplemented the program with in-store promotions and coupons distributed through Facebook and print to encourage their target markets to try the product. It was a multimedia effort designed to reach and engage their target market and move them to like them on Facebook and tell others about the video. As you will see, they accomplished these results in stellar fashion.

Entertain Them

While this program was a success from the first posting of the video on YouTube and Facebook, Old Spice and Weiden+Kennedy present a best-of-breed example of how to entertain and further engage a target market using Engagement Marketing. As the initial video and subsequent ones went viral, people began to discuss them on Twitter and Facebook. Weiden+Kennedy enhanced the program by asking people to submit questions to the Manly Man. They then did something that shows the power of social. They worked day and night and quickly shot responses to the best questions. These responses made Old Spice unique and demonstrated the power of social to engage a target market, even though they don't know them on a personal, one-on-one basis. Watch their video responses by clicking on the picture or by going to this page on YouTube: http://youtu.be/fD1WqPGn5Ag.[18]

Old Spice – The Man your Man could Smell Like campaign
Uploaded August 2010 Wieden + Kennedy Portland case
link http://youtu.be/fD1WqPGn5Ag

Strengthen the Relationship

As the initial effort went viral, Old Spice and Weiden+Kennedy were ready with a series of other videos. Remember, you only have a relatively short period of time to be Awesome so, by following one awesome video with another, Weiden+Kennedy was able to keep the buzz going. Their target markets eagerly awaited every new video and virally responded to each one. This grew the organization's social footprint as well as the size of their virally attuned market. [http://vimeo.com/47875656]

They even had Isaiah talk in chat rooms (https://www.youtube.com/watch?v=5zxC5d8iux8) and then had some fun showing how they made the commercials on cable TV and in chat rooms. They had fun with the concept and with the fame resulting from the successful program.

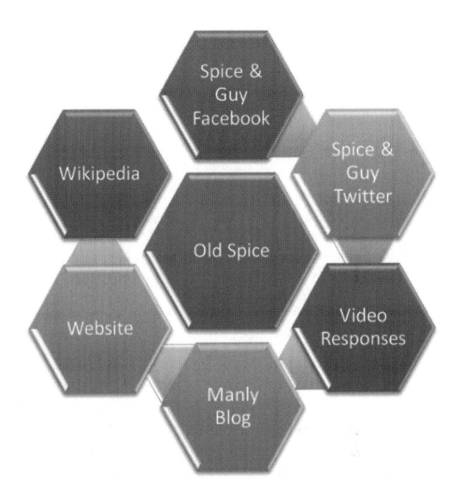

In addition to the new videos, Old Spice used all types of social media to engage their target market and expand their social footprint. They quickly created social entities in a variety of sites used by their target market. They used both the Old Spice social assets along with those created specifically for the Manly Man. The goal was to make it easy for the target market to find the Manly Man, to have fun with him, and to experience the awesome video content created to engage and sell them on making their man smell like a man.

What Were the Results?

From all social metrics, the "Manly Man" campaign was a monster success. They had over forty million views and about a hundred and fifty-eight thousand Facebook likes. Their Twitter following rose at triple-digit rates. This case study video, cited in the last bullet point, is a great way to see the final results of the effort. Impressive.

Old Spice – The Man your Man could Smell Like campaign
Uploaded August 2010 Wieden + Kennedy Portland case
link http://youtu.be/fD1WqPGn5Ag

Did it work? The Old Spice example shows the impact viral activity can have on an Engagement Marketing program. When they released their first "Manly Man" ads, by the end of day one (day one!), it had over 5.9 million views. By day two, it held eight out of the top eleven spots of most popular views on the web. By the end of day three, the ads had over twenty million views.[19] Today, it eclipses forty million views! Click on the graphic or here to view the results (http://youtu.be/fD1WqPGn5Ag).

Beyond YouTube, the Awesome content impacted all of the organization's social networking sites. Because they used Twitter to both monitor fan reactions and to engage with them in clever ads answering their questions, the organization's Twitter following grew by 2700 percent. Their Facebook fan interaction grew by over 800 percent and traffic on their organization website—OldSpice.com—grew by over 300 percent.

Beyond their social network, the "Manly Man" program generated impressions on other media as well. The ads were mentioned by Oprah, CNN, the Today show, and a large number of local and national news programs. At six months after launch, the "Manly Man" Engagement Marketing program had created over 1.4 billion impressions on other media. It became one of the most talked-about advertisements of all time.

Did the program generate sales? Definitely—but it's difficult to prove conclusively. Six months after the "Manly Man" program began, sales were up 27 percent, by nine months were up 55 percent, and after ten months were up 107 percent. These are impressive numbers. However, generating these sales was actually a combination of marketing efforts by Old Spice. As *Adweek* noted, while the "Manly Man" ads were a significant social component, couponing, in-store efforts, and other brand and marketing investments also played a key role in the growth of the brand. Regardless, Old Spice is a master in their use of the Social Engagement strategy to impact and engage their broad, young target market.

Old Spice "Manly Man" Summary

The Old Spice campaign shows the power of Engagement Marketing. With a relatively new product, Old Spice launched an integrated Engagement Marketing program that became one of the biggest of all time. It was one of the most successful launches in the category and grew the organization's social footprint, distributed coupons, and helped drive sales. It's one of the best examples of Engagement Marketing.

There is one other thing to learn from the Old Spice example. In 2013, Old Spice and other companies attempted to use a similar strategy for their new product launches. While they are going well, they're nowhere near the popularity of this original program. Why? One of the challenges of Engagement Marketing is to be truly original. When you use a strategy employed for another product or by another organization, the viral reaction is weak. The attitude of the social cloud is, "Been there, done that." To really grow your social footprint, originality and being viewed as awesome by the target market are keys to success. If you appear to be a derivative strategy, your results will be weak. Engagement Marketing seeks the new and entertaining, so plan to give it to them.

Cadbury Dairy Milk Group

Cadbury Chocolates—a UK organization—has been using exceptional Engagement Marketing programs for years. They are a great example of focused, long-term Engagement Marketing designed to steadily grow their social footprint and then, after it had grown, developing Engagement Marketing strategies to maximize their involvement with Cadbury over time.

In 2010 and '11, Cadbury and their Cadbury Dairy Milk group began aggressively deploying their Engagement Marketing strategy. Their goal was to achieve one million Likes on Facebook. They also wanted to engage with their social site fans over time to maintain the engagement and make Cadbury chocolate in the top of the minds of the members of their target markets.

Target Broadly

Cadbury's target market was people who love chocolate. This is a passion market in which your passions somewhat negate your demographic profile. Whether you are young or old, rich or poor, if you had a love for chocolate, Cadbury's was the place to go to satisfy your chocolate passion.

Even though they're a UK organization, Cadbury's Engagement Marketing strategies were internationally focused. They wanted members from all over the world to participate on their Facebook pages and to become a part of the Cadbury community. The focus was on your passion for chocolate … not a specific demographic characteristic.

Create Awesome

Cadbury is one of the best at creating Awesome content. From early in 2010, the organization began creating and distributing Awesome content using different types of social media. On their Facebook page, they continually added new articles, recipes, and videos about people creating things using chocolate. They also sponsored a number of contests to challenge their networking visitors to use chocolate in interesting and fun ways. These contests and some of their interestng projects helped Cadbury add new members virally to grow toward its goal of one million followers on Facebook.

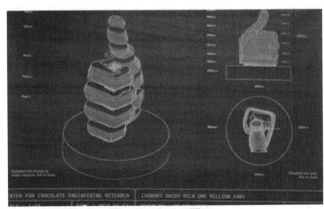

Cadbury Dairy Milk – Thanks A Million
Uploaded Aug 2012 link http://youtu.be/uHtDRw4ujYw

Cadbury found social networking was an excellent way to grow a community of people passionate about chocolate. To accomplish their goal of one million Likes, they executed a number of great Engagement Marketing programs targeted at specific groups of people with chocolate passions. They introduced chocolate recipes, had games involving chocolate to attract younger people, built cars and other items using chocolate, and did other fun activities designed to engage people with a passion for chocolate.

Go Viral

Cadbury Dairy Milk – Joyville Site
http://joyville.cadbury.com.au/

Cadbury promoted its Facebook page in print, on its products, and using PR efforts. Their Awesome video content quickly went viral among wide communities. Each effort created buzz that allowed Cadbury's Diary Milk site to grow to over one million members in a very short period of time—and it's still growing. Note that now it's over seven million. Having content that was awesome, meaningful, and visual made it a hit among chocolate lovers. The organization's content often went viral and quickly grew their social footprint on Facebook and elsewhere.

They also used their website and other sites to tell people about their forty-eight-hour celebration. In the messages, they gave the individual a way to learn more about their live streaming video celebrating their one million Facebook fans. They gave you a way to become a participant, become a Facebook follower, and tell your friends about it. Cadbury used social, web, and traditional marketing to reach chocolate lovers and invite them to the celebration.

Entertain Them

Throughout their celebration, Cadbury asked their live viewers and their friends on Facebook and Twitter to engage with the organization. If you watch their video (click on the picture of the thumb), you'll see a Community Notice Board behind the thumb where they posted notes of encouragement, congratulations, and other messages from their Facebook community. During the forty-eight hour build, they also drank hot cocoa, made celebration cakes, and had activities and contests designed to involve their community.[20]

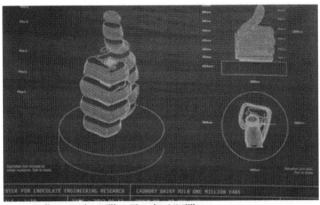

Cadbury Dairy Milk – Thanks A Million
Uploaded Aug 2012 link http://youtu.be/uHtDRw4ujYw

When they completed their Facebook thumb, and the streaming video had ended, Cadbury used the experience for one more demonstration of their social consciousness. They took their giant thumb and sold the chocolate to raise funds for an organization specializing in renewable fuels. From start to finish, Cadbury's entire program was a fun way to celebrate chocolate, the organization's Facebook success and, in the end, helped advance research in an important area to help the planet.

Strengthen the Relationship

While Cadbury Dairy Milk quickly achieved its social goals, there was an issue. The organization had achieved its goal of one million Facebook Likes, but research found only 16 percent of its one million Facebook fans actually looked at content posted on their Facebook site.[21] To increase engagement, Dairy Milk brand manager Sarah Lindley created the Joyville marketing activity. It was designed to seed content on social to build buzz among its online community before turning to TV and print channels. While the Joyville adventure and activities are now closed, you can still visit their site by clicking on the graphic. It shows a great way to strengthen the relationship with your new fans while increasing engagement in a measurable way.

Cadbury Dairy Milk – Thanks A Million
Showing the Comment Wall

What Were the Results?

Did it work? Cadbury Dairy Milk achieved over one million Likes on their Facebook page. This resulted in the forty-eight-hour celebration, during which they built a Facebook "Like thumb" using three English tonnes of chocolate. While the event was happening, Cadbury recorded over three hundred and fifty thousand people involved in the campaign, and the organization gained over forty thousand new Facebook fans! The more important result reported by Dairy Milk brand manager Sarah Lindley was an increase in Facebook participation from 16 percent to over 33 percent because of this and other events.[22]

Cadbury Dairy Milk Summary

For companies wanting to use Engagement Marketing to attract and maintain engagement with their target markets, Sarah Lindley told David Roth of Econsultancy the following:

Cadbury Dairy Milk – Thanks A Million Infographic
http://www.digitalbuzzblog.com/wp-content/uploads/2012/01/Cadbury-Infographic.jpg

"Cadbury found that the best way to increase reach on Facebook is to offer fans a big reward for minimum effort on their part. While core fans may engage with all your content, to get their friends to become engaged it has to be extremely easy for them to interact."

Lindley said she would highly recommend experimenting with Facebook to see what can be achieved, but it should be supported with media buys to raise awareness and see how far it can be pushed.[23] We agree. This infographic shows the results of their Engagement Marketing strategy back in 2011.[24] An effective use of Engagement Marketing to grow the social footprint of Cadbury Dairy Milk. [http://www.digitalbuzzblog.com/wp-content/uploads/2012/01/Cadbury-Infographic.jpg]

Engagement Marketing Summary

Regardless of whether it was a focused or multifaceted program, companies using the Engagement Marketing strategy have some common characteristics:

- **Focus on Social Networks:** All of these examples were executed using Facebook, Twitter, or other social networks as the main delivery mechanisms for the strategy. While they may have discussed it on their organization blogs, used banner ads, promoted it on the web, or advertised it in print media, these examples were delivered through networking systems. This allowed the organization to have the broadest market impact that results in the greatest likelihood that it will go viral for the organization.

- **Anonymous Relationships:** While the Engagement Marketing examples had dialog with their viewers/participants, they were anonymous relationships. While that did not stop the companies from having fun and engaging with different individuals, they really did not know nor did they retain anything about them. While the next two social strategies are built on developing one-on-one, database-driven relationships, Engagement Marketing is socially focused and does not need knowledge of the individual to drive the strategy forward.

- **Internal Social Networking Measures:** In all of these examples, you did not hear about ROI, profits or growth in sales. This is because a Social Engagement strategy is measured by internal metrics like the increase in Likes, Friends and Followers. Look yourself at all of the best-of-breed Social Engagement campaigns. They're all measured in terms of these internal metrics.

5

The Nurture Marketing Strategy

Compared to Engagement Marketing, Nurture Marketing takes relationships to the next level. In Engagement Marketing, the relationship is anonymous, and the strategy is focused on exciting a broad market to friend the organization and grow the organization's social footprint. Nurture Marketing is different. It will focus on a specific, high-value market you want to develop. It will then engage the targeted prospect with highly relevant content to elicit a response. Their response builds a database that allows for a one-to-one relationship with each individual—and much more.

The Nurture Marketing strategy is the first of our three strategies that link social media to your organization's sales and marketing systems. This means we know—in real time—if individuals are prospects, customers, or past and inactive customers with your organization. We'll also be able to monitor and best determine their interests and where they are in their product purchase lifecycle. This allows for targeted communications to move them to the next level in our relationship. Finally, because we can link to our sales and marketing systems, we can actually monitor our marketing expenditures for social and traditional marketing to revenue generation and profits. Nurture

Marketing allows you to show senior management the revenues, profits and Return on Investment (ROI) of your organization's social media investment. It links your social investment to the KPIs (Key Performance Indicators) driving your organization.

Developing and Deploying a Nurture Marketing Strategy

Effective Nurture Marketing programs are built using a five-step process. Like all integrated marketing efforts, it starts with a high value target market and develops content relevant to each market. The relevant content is then delivered through the market channel preferred by the individuals in the target market. The steps are:

Target Interests

To build a successful Nurture Marketing strategy, you need to understand the needs, interests and aspirations of a specific target market. You're not interested in viral activity (although that is a nice plus) but want to provide them with content of relevance and entice them

to engage with your organization. What this means is that you not only need to deeply understand the personas of your high-value target markets, you also need to know the topics of importance to them. To determine hot topics, you need to add social monitoring to your market analysis.

To develop a Nurture Marketing program, you need to do all of the targeting steps defined in the Engagement Marketing strategy. You need to size and value your target markets, and evaluate them in terms of the sites they tend to go to find expert information. In Engagement Marketing, the goal is a broad target market capable of going viral. In Nurture Marketing, the key is identifying unique markets and the topics of interest to them. If two or more target markets are attracted to a specific hot topic, you'll want to separate them in the registration process.

How can you identify the topics of interest to your target markets? First, analyze your target audiences and use descriptive information to establish a persona of the archetype individual or business you want to develop. Try to make the persona as rich as possible in terms of their defining characteristics.

When you develop the persona of a high value audience, there are often gaps. These gaps represent interest, lifestyle, product interest and other information you would like to know. To fill in those blank areas, the Nurture Strategy offers two solutions. The first is you can ask them and the second is we can gather that information as we build a relationship with them. This is a technique called progressive profiling. Because Nurture Marketing is an ever-growing relationship captured on your organization's social database, we can add to our understanding of the target audience by observing their habits on our website and social assets, asking them questions using surveys and other techniques, or by engaging with them individually to answer questions and concerns. With Nurture Marketing, your goal is to continually grow your knowledge of your target audience as they engage with you within the strategy.

In addition to developing a persona description, it is also very useful to learn the social habits of your target audience. To accomplish this, you can survey them and ask them how they use social media, who they consider experts and key sources of information related to your products and services, and where they go when they are gathering information to make a purchase decision. While surveying can give you these insights, there is another way to learn about your target audience. That is using social monitoring tools.

Social monitoring tools are designed to listen to social chatter on specific topics. These topics can be your organization and your competitors, topics related to your business, specific individuals, the products and services you sell, and any other topic you want to analyze. These systems are designed to go to all of the levels in the social pyramid discussed in chapter two and actively listen for what you want to know. Pay-per-use systems like Radian6, Crimson Hexagon, the IBM social monitoring system and Netbase are useful because they can listen to social chatter over time and give you a historical perspective. However, if you are getting started, there are three free systems that can provide you key information you can use to build your Nurture Marketing strategy.

Social Mention (www.socialmention.com) is one of the most useful free social monitoring tools you can use. It's designed to allow you to analyze and track social conversations on any topic of relevance to your organization. You can track conversations about your organization, your products and services, and your competitors, and can track them over time to identify changes in the social chatter. You can also track the topics related to your organization and your offerings that are being discussed right now in the social cloud.

Beyond showing you important information on key topics, the site also gives you the hash tags people are using on Twitter to discuss the topic, the sites in the social pyramid they are using to engage with each other, keywords they're using to define the topic, and people who are most active in the conversation. This free site gives you key insights and information you can incorporate directly into your social marketing program(s). One more thing—Social Mention can be used internationally using the advanced search option!

AllTop (www.alltop.com) stands for All Topics and is designed to find the most current articles and sites in real-time. It's a great site to use to find the current articles being written about topics of interest to you. With Alltop you can enter a topic and it will show you sites containing recent articles. The sites are arranged from most influential on down to allow you to focus on the most important articles within your search. AllTop is a great way to find additional articles for your virtual community pages or your organization's website. It's also useful to keep you up to date on the articles your customers and prospects are reading on key topics.

We Follow (www.wefollow.com) is a third useful social monitoring site. In the discussion of any topic, there are key individuals at the center of the conversation. You need to know who they are, what they're saying, and their potential to assist your social program. These individuals often reach hundreds, thousands, or even millions of readers.

Like the other social monitoring systems, you enter a topic, and We Follow will show you a list of business and individuals who are influential in the discussion. The most influential organization/individual gets a score of 100 and others are ranked from 100 to 0. You should identify the most influential individuals, see their number of followers, and begin following them. In all of the social strategies, if you can get an influencer excited and they tell their followers, you have amplified your message in the exact target market you want to develop. Take some time to develop a list of the most influential people, and it will pay benefits for every one of your social efforts.

Create Relevance

To engage with your target market, you need to create content that is highly relevant to them. Using your target market analyses, you have learned the topics of interest to them and the topics where you can positively contribute to the conversation. In the Create Relevance  step, you want to create content that will be so useful, they will want to engage with you to get it.

In the Nurture Marketing strategy, this content can be developed in a variety of formats. Your content could be developed into an e-book, a white paper, a video you can place on your private organization channel, a great tool, or even a mobile app. If your content helps your target market work more effectively or addresses one of their needs, it's a great candidate to become the focal point for your Nurture Marketing effort. Not sure? You might give several options to influential bloggers or customers you know are in the target market to get their advice.

When considering what content to develop, keep in mind passion and trigger event communities will have different informational needs. Passion markets want content that is new, interesting, and unique. For passion markets, consider having a webinar with trend-setting experts, a short video from an expert on a new trend or technology, or a short, focused article on a topic of interest to them. Monitor your social networks or talk to your customers in the target market and determine the hot topics and trends of interest to their passion group. Then develop content that appeals to them.

One of my clients is a manufacturer of components used in computers and similar technologies. Their target audience is CEOs of major companies in specific verticals who are passionate about the newest ideas to improve their organization. This organization developed a series of periodic webinars on new management trends and techniques. These webinars are not designed to sell the organization's products and services but rather appeal and attract CEOs and CFOs interested in keeping abreast of issues. When they find a hot topic, they create a webinar and market it using the Nurture Marketing Strategy.

For a trigger-event market, keep in mind they're on a quest or mission that has been traveled by others before them. For this group, how-to articles, videos, and webinars are great ways to develop content. For example, one organization who wanted to attract new brides (a trigger event) ran a series of webinars with cable stars and other experts on different challenges when planning a wedding. One was about getting the right wedding gown, another was on planning the reception.. Because they were very helpful for the brides, they were widely attended and the recordings were extensively watched even years later. Because this trigger market moves quickly from proposal to wedding, the organization is continues developing new webinars as well as updating older ones to keep them relevant.

In Engagement Marketing, once you have the content, you place it on your video and social networking assets to begin engaging the target market. In the Nurture Marketing strategy, the process is very different. You are designing content that is highly relevant to a specific target market. It's designed to address their needs or provide them with useful information that is within your areas of expertise. To make it work in a Nurture Marketing strategy, you're going to place it behind a wall. You don't want to just give it to the target audience. You want to use it as an enticement for an information exchange. The exchange is, "You give me key information about yourself, your organization (if B2B), and your needs, and in return, I will give some great relevant content to help you." To accomplish this, you want to first take your prospect to a landing page.

Site Optimization for E-Commerce Companies:
See How Leading Online Brands Are Converting Browser into Buyers

With the online retail sector growing quickly, so is the competition for that increased revenue and growth. Now more than ever, online retailers recognize that it's not only vital to drive shoppers to their sites, but also to ensure that they stay and make online purchases in growing numbers.

The key to increased conversions is optimizing the online customer experience — and what was once an art, is now just as much a science.

By leveraging the latest optimization technology, leading online e-commerce companies are now dynamically testing content, graphics, offers, layout, and functionality to gain new insight into the experiences their site visitors prefer.

They're seeing what works and what doesn't — using valuable data from their testing to make site changes to improve the online shopping experience, increase customer loyalty, and convert more browsers into buyers.

Learn more by downloading this free e-book today.

This content is published by:

Register now to get your copy of this research! FREE!

* is a required field

First Name *
Last Name *
Work Email *
Job Title *
Company *
Phone Number *
Address *

City *
State * Select a State
Zip/Postal Code *
Country * Select a Country

Would you like to be added to SiteSpect's monthly optimization newsletter? * ☐ Yes ☐ No

Would you like to see a demo of SiteSpect's non-intrusive optimization platform? * ☐ Yes ☐ No

SUBMIT

Please note that any information you supply is protected by our privacy policy.

A landing page generally has two sides. On the left is information about the offer and what the reader will receive. On the right is the information exchange section. The information exchange is generally separated into two types of data—required data and optional data.

In the Nurture Marketing strategy, one of your goals is to create a database of information on each person requesting the Relevant Content. To accomplish this, you need—at minimum—their e-mail address. By itself, the email address allows you to track subsequent downloads, allows you to overlay the file with address and descriptive information, and gives you a link to your sales and marketing systems. Beyond e-mail address, you can also require name and address fields, organization and title information, and any other data that would help your organization in building a relationship. BUT keep in mind that too much information results in lowered number of completions. Balance is the key.

Optional information can be questions or additional data elements you would like to obtain. From experience, it's often better to make most data elements optional. The majority of people will complete nearly all of the form anyway. Keep in mind the more information you make mandatory, the more likely it is visitors will wonder why you need all this data.

At the bottom of the landing page are several data elements extremely important to your success. These are the Opt-in/ Opt-out data fields. Most people are leery of providing data to an organization. To help alleviate this concern, give them control of the marketing process through your opt-in buttons. Tell them what you want to do and let them tell you what they give you permission to do. This will set the tone of the conversation and will give individuals peace of mind about downloading or accessing your relevant content.

As they complete their registration process and click the enter button, two things happen. First, companies using the Nurture Marketing strategy place a tracking cookie on the individual's computer. This allows the organization to track the visitor's activities on the organization website and some social sites, and it lets them know when someone requests additional information. Second, the organization sends the individual an e-mail allowing them access to the Relevant Content. Why do this? It makes sure the e-mail they provided you is accurate. You then know you have an accurate link to use in building your database. If it bounces, eliminate the record from your database. You can't contact them and they can't get to your relevant content. If they really want it, they can reregister.

Go Fishing

When teaching this strategy, it was a struggle to give this step a name but Go Fishing is very apt. Each year, my son and I used to go fishing in Canada. The lakes we fished contained northern pike and walleye—two very different kinds of fish. Each day we had to determine  what fish we wanted to catch, because the same lures would not work for both types of fish. What you fished with determined what you caught. We would start with a preferred lure then, if no fish were caught after a period of time, we would switch to a different lure. The key was to use our knowledge of the fish and their tendencies and our knowledge of fishing lures to find the exact right lure to attract the fish. Find the right combination and you would fill your stringer with fish.

To a certain extent, this is an analogy for developing your Go Fishing marketing program. Your goal is to develop a marketing program that appears on the social and traditional marketing channels used by your target market. You need to inform them of your new, relevant content and entice them to click through to the landing page.

As with any type of marketing, you need to test different communications to find the one that best engages your target market and moves them to the landing page to request your content.

To deploy your Nurture Marketing program, you want to use all of the marketing channels preferred by your target market. While this varies for different companies, some you'll want to consider include banner ads, communities on social sites like Google+ and LinkedIn, e-journals and e-newsletters, Twitter, and pay-per-click. You should also e-mail the target market members on your organization's database and procure e-mail lists of prospects. The key is to widely promote your relevant content to move your target market to your landing page.

Classify

As discussed earlier, when people register to receive your information, you place them in your database. To build a relationship with them, you need to identify three things. One is who are they? The second is what products and services interest them? The third is where are they in the purchase cycle?

When individuals first register to receive your relevant content, you have only a little information to develop their persona classification. You might use the source where they came from, and the information provided on the form to attempt to classify them into a persona segment. In addition, unless the content was very product specific, you will only have a general understanding of their product interests and their point in the product purchase lifecycle.

When Silverpop's clients overviewed their Nurture Marketing methodology, they stressed the importance of viewing the classification process as an incremental process. You probably have only a little information at the point of registration. As you match new responders to your sales and marketing systems using their e-mail addresses, you separate the customers from the prospects. In the case of customers, you can learn the products they purchased and, often, their persona classification. If you overlay all of the new respondents with descriptive demographic and life style data, you can classify them even more accurately.

The identification of the persona, product, and product lifecycle stage of each of your new registrants becomes extremely powerful when you look at their real-time behaviors. Remember the cookies you placed on their computer? Every time they visit your website, you can learn the pages they were examining, the articles they were reading, and other site-specific behaviors to refine your knowledge base of them. If they download additional content, especially content developed for specific stages in the lifecycle, you can become even more refined in your knowledge. With each action, your knowledge grows and you have a better understanding of their needs, interests, and place in the product purchase lifecycle.

Nurture

The goal of the Nurture process is straightforward. Move registrants to the next step in the product purchase lifecycle. This is accomplished by giving them tailored content developed for their persona segment's needs and product interests. The content will be designed to give  them the information, insights, and knowledge necessary to make it easy to move to the next step in the process.

Product Purchase Lifecycle

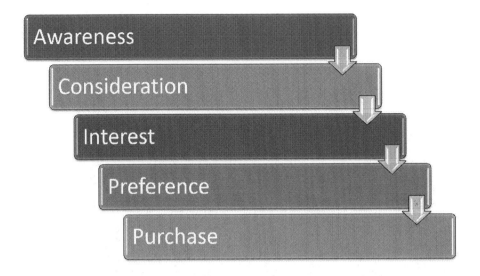

How do you know what to offer? You don't, but because you're measuring every contact and every content offering you are making, you can test different content to determine the one that best attracts and engages each persona segment. You will be watching whether they download new content offerings, examine what they're seeking when they visit your websites, monitor to see if they're engaging with you through live chat or discussions with your sales force, and all of your other monitored touch points. From this knowledge, you can continually assess each individual and determine the best content to deliver to them next. It's a continual learning and testing process.

Nurture Marketing Results Metrics

Nurture Marketing is measured in four ways. First, you can use social metrics to gauge how it is increasing your social footprint. In this strategy, your goal is not just to get an individual in a targeted, high-value market to respond to your content offer, but also to have them 1) join your social network and 2) tell others about your offer. If the content is relevant and helpful, both activities will occur. You should see an increase in most of your social media as well as some viral activity as the engaged individual tells their friends about your content.

A second key set of metrics is the effectiveness and efficiency of your acquisition content offering(s). In the acquisition cycle, you'll be advertising your content on banner ads, PPC campaigns, your website, your social sites, and with communities where your target market resides. You will also e-mail customers and prospects in the targeted markets as well. The metrics in the acquisition cycle are designed to determine which sources are most effective in generating click-through behaviors to the landing page, which messages are most effective in producing these clicks, and how effective your landing page is in getting them to enter their information accurately and click to receive their content. You'll do a great deal of message testing for each acquisition program to ensure you are reaching your targeted market.

The third set of metrics is the start of the progressive profiling you will use throughout the Nurture program. Once an individual responds, you'll want to classify them by market segment. You will also classify them in terms of the products they're likely to be considering and the likely time until their first purchase.

This data is used to drive your nurture program. The nurture program is designed to create a structured series of messages to move each individual from suspect to prospect to customer. This nurture program is measured in much the same way as integrated marketing programs using more traditional marketing channels. You will want to know the number sent, opened and read, the number who respond to content and offers, and the number who move through to first purchase. As individuals move down the product purchase lifecycle, you would anticipate greater numbers of first time sales. The metric program will measure to see if that is occurring and will tell you which of your nurture program elements is working effectively to build a stronger relationship.

The final set of metrics are the traditional business metrics. The Nurture Marketing strategy is the first one that can track activities from your social offerings through to first purchase and beyond. When an individual first responds to a Nurture Marketing offer, you can match their record by e-mail or address to see if they are a current or past customer. Because you know what was invested to acquire and nurture each individual, the number making their first or repeat purchases and the amounts they're spending, you can take this data and develop a set of standard business metrics. You can create profitability and other KPIs (Key Performance Indicators) like Return on Investment (ROI), number of months to recover the marketing investment, and breakeven to develop and justify new programs and to grow current ones.

Because you're targeting specific target markets and you know your current market share, you can add new prospects gained from the Nurture Marketing program(s) to show growth in your market share. After the Nurture Marketing programs are established, you can look at active customers who were and were not participants in your Nurture Marketing efforts. This allows you to show the incremental strength social plays in increasing lifetime value. The key is Nurture Marketing is the first of two strategies that provides a direct link between your social marketing investment and bottom-line revenues and profits.

Strategy Limitations

Designing, developing, and deploying an effective Nurture Marketing strategy costs time and resources. As a result, it should only be used in your high-value/high-opportunity markets. You need to have the revenue flow and market size to make it effective. You need a strong market to justify this type of program.

A second limitation is that the Nurture Marketing strategy works best for companies who have a number of steps in their product purchase lifecycle. This does not mean it's only for B2B applications. If there are multiple steps between awareness and final purchase, a Nurture Marketing program will work for you. Most products have multiple steps, so this strategy can also be used for B2C.

Another limitation is it's a reactionary strategy. Nurture Marketing does not grab your high value markets and isolate them from the competition. It trolls for people who are interested, and then attempts to build a nurturing relationship with them. As a result, it may only reach a part of your total market. Nurture Marketing programs are great ways to use social to augment and drive your social strategy. They do work well with other lead generation programs. Keep in mind that it only starts when the targeted prospect takes the first action.

Best Applications

Nurture Marketing strategies are useful in any situation where the individual is attracted to relevant information and can then be moved toward a purchase. For some clients, the journey from prospect to customer is relatively short. For others, it takes months or even years for an individual to move from suspect to prospect to customer. The great strength of the Nurture Marketing strategy is its ability to monitor individual interactions over time with your organization and identify when there is interest or movement toward a potential purchase. It's marketing by offering relevant content tailored to the product purchase lifecycle and then observing your target markets to see their interests and determine their needs.

Nurture Marketing appears to be strongest in situations where the selling process is somewhat complex. Business-to-business marketing often has many steps in the product purchase lifecycle and requires the involvement of different management and professional levels to make the sale. These types of selling situations are best suited to a Nurture Marketing approach.

The same is true for consumer marketing of complex or costly products. If the product requires education and different types of information to sell the individual, Nurture Marketing is a great way to initiate the relationship and support it throughout the purchase process. The database and your observations of their interactions gives you the insights you need to most effectively move them from prospect to customer.

Nurture Marketing Summary

Unlike the Engagement Marketing strategy, Nurture Marketing is designed to engage, monitor, and interact with individuals to move them from prospect to customer. It's designed to attract the target market to your site, and give them relevant information to start the relationship. It also does two more things. It presents them with additional content you think move them forward in the product purchase lifecycle and then monitors their interactions to determine if they're showing signs of moving toward purchase.

Engagement Marketing	Nurture Marketing
Target Broadly	Target Interests
Create Awesome	Create Relevant
Go Social	"Go Fishing"
Entertain	Classify
Strengthen	Nurture

Because the Nurture Marketing strategy develops a database of all target market individuals attracted to your Relevant Content offerings, it allows your organization to track the relationship from social interaction through to product purchase. It gives you the ability to measure your Nurture Marketing investment against actual purchase revenues from your sales and marketing systems. It gives you a total picture of the individual's relationship and the value of the target market to your bottom-line profits.

Comparing the Nurture Marketing and the Engagement Marketing strategies, it's easy to see the strong marketing focus of Nurture Marketing. Nurture Marketing is a strategy that is very useful for most organizations and companies—from start-ups to Fortune 100. It gives you the ability to integrate social activities into a database-driven marketing system for your high-value markets..

6

Nurture Marketing Strategy Case Studies

The two case studies in this chapter were selected because they show the Nurture Marketing strategy in two situations. The first is using Nurture Marketing in a business-to-business relationship. The second is a deployment of the strategy in a consumer relationship. Unlike the Engagement Marketing cases, these two were developed through direct engagement with the organizations and the technology companies which supplied them the capabilities to develop and execute a Nurture Marketing program. As with the other strategies, as we become aware of new cases, we will add them to the book's website at www.SocialIMC.com.

NetProspex

NetProspex is an organization dedicated to providing smarter data to drive marketing programs.[25] While the organization is a successful and growing organization, it wanted to accelerate its growth using a Nurture Marketing strategy. They contacted Silverpop, a digital marketing technology provider that unifies marketing automation, e-mail, mobile, and social.[26] Ellen Valentine, Product Evangelist at Silverpop, is a key thought leader in how to deploy Nurture Marketing Strategies.

Silverpop worked with a number of companies to help NetProspex develop, deploy, and benefit from their Nurture Marketing program.

According to Silverpop and NetProspex, in 2011 NetProspex had a major problem. In reviewing their sales and marketing systems, they found their website was very organization centric, had little content of interest to their highest value prospects, and their sales and marketing systems did not help prospects move through the product purchase lifecycle. Based on their analysis, they established a series of organizational and marketing goals. Specifically, NetProspex wanted to:

- Better understand their buyers and their journey (the product purchase life cycle).
- Develop the personas of their most valuable prospects.
- Build up a library of relevant content to help them through their journey.
- Develop and deploy a Nurture Marketing strategy to acquire, classify, and nurture the respondents.
- Link these marketing programs to the sales database to track the relationship from the information exchange through to the final sale.

The organization also established a series of social and business metrics as goals for the program. They wanted to witness increased visitation to the site, increased duration of stays on their site, a reduction in the bounce rate for their e-mail communications, and an increase in conversions (sales). Each goal was quantified to allow the organization to manage and adjust their Nurture Marketing programs to reach their goals. While I will not present the initial goal metrics, I will show their final, actual results at the end of this section.

Target Interests

In analyzing the journey of their buyers, they found they needed to impact three distinct markets. The first was called Demand Gen. These were managers involved with generating demand for their organization's products and services. They managed acquisition and relationship marketing programs. The second market was Operations managers. These were IT and operations specialists who managed data and data acquisition. This group would house and provide access to NetProspex's data. The final target market was sales leadership. These were individuals who were on the front lines of the sales process and needed accurate descriptive data to help them develop their sales approaches.

For each of these markets, NetProspex found a difference between technical and nontechnical individuals. The technical ones liked the process and the details of how the data was collected, updated, stored, and used. Nontechnical individuals wanted to know applications and results from using the data, not the process required to get it. They found the level of technical prowess impacted the type of content each market wanted and needed.

In the targeting step, NetProspex developed a detailed description of each target market and established a persona to represent each segment. Christina is an example of a Technical Demand Generator. Notice the detailed description and how they are linking descriptive and motivational data to develop a comprehensive understanding of this target audience. By developing personas, your organization is positioned to create the relevant content you need to engage and acquire them for your Nurture program.

Create Relevance

In developing their relevant content, NetProspex created different types of content items. They created content designed to appeal to each persona category's unique data and information needs. They then built more content designed to move each persona group through their product purchase lifecycle. Some items would be tested to acquire each persona segment. Others were designed to move each segment through their product life cycle. Once the organization knew where you were in making the data purchase decision, they would nurture you with custom developed content designed to answer your immediate questions and move you to the next stage in the product purchase decision. This content was placed behind a registration wall. Individuals wanting to get the content had to complete a form that provided key information to NetProspex marketers. NetProspex asked questions about the organization and the title of the individual who wanted their content.

Go Fishing

NetProspex used a multichannel approach to attract and engage their high value target markets. They prospected using social messages, banner advertisements, website announcements, and similar channels. For target prospects currently on the organization's marketing system, they used e-mail to tell them about their relevant content. Together, they reached out to their high value target markets to attract them to the registration landing page.

Classify

Once individuals responded and downloaded the content material, their landing site entries were captured, and each individual was assigned to a persona segment. Based on their persona and past engagements (if any) with the organization, their most likely products and probable place in the purchase lifecycle was determined. This assignment was altered as new site use, content download, and social activities were added to their database record. Each assessment placed the individual into the nurture channel best suited to them. From their persona segment and position in the product purchase lifecycle, the nurture program could begin. For each segment, the organization developed a number of steps in the life cycle. Three are shown here: Engage, Propensity, and Decision.

Nurture

The content below illustrates the Nurture program they developed for their markets. On the graphic, you see NetProspex segmented their target market into three persona segments. They were individuals interested in Demand Generation, Data Management and Sales Prospecting. They could determine this from their job title, type of organization they worked at, and information generated by matching individuals with their sales and marketing files.

The product purchase lifecycle is displayed in the three big boxes in the center of the graphic. NetProspex determined they could assess each persona segment in the three steps of Engage, Propensity, and Decision.

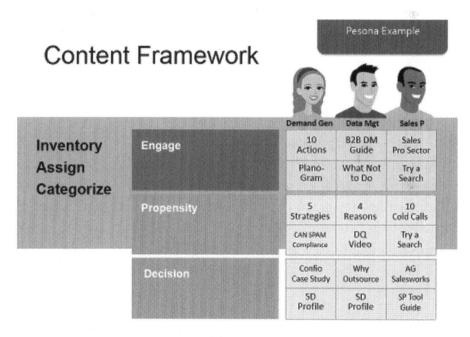

For each step in the lifecycle and each persona segment, NetProspex created two different types of content. They have articles, guides, and videos for each persona segment. The engagement level is mostly informational. The propensity level has content designed to convince. Notice they have terms like *five strategies*, *four reasons*, and *try a search*—all experiences designed to convince and move you into purchase mode.

The decision level contains case studies, rationales for outsourcing your data series and a tool guide. All are designed to make it easy to choose NetProspex as your data provider.

In their Nurture program, each response or lack of response leads to the next offer in the chain. Because the system is constantly measuring the results of each step in the chain, systems like Silverpop can immediately measure results and, based on a time sequence, execute the next step in the Nurture strategy. Each step is automatic, highly personalized, and tailored to the individual and their stage in the product purchase lifecycle.

What Were the Results?

In the first few months of their program, the NetProspex witnessed a 12.5 times increase in the visit duration from their target markets. In addition, most persona targets doubled in the number of pages they visited on the site. They also saw a 30 percent reduction in the number of bounces from their messages. Their messages were getting through to the right individual, being opened, and content was being read on the site.

Beyond e-mail metrics, the organization saw a 4.7 percent increase in conversions. This means increased sales. While I cannot release the actual sales results, the organization is seeing increased purchases in their highest value persona segments. By tailoring each communication and nurturing each prospect as they move through their product purchase life cycle, NetProspex is showing the way using Nurture Marketing to build their market share where they most wanted to develop.

NetProspex Summary

The NetProspex case shows you the power and targeting capability of the Nurture Marketing strategy. For each unique persona they wanted to attract, they created two different content offerings for each of the three steps in their product purchase lifecycle. Keep in mind that each of these content offerings could be used as the initial acquisition article to attract prospects to the registration page or could be targeted to individuals once they were in the Nurture system. By having two content offerings per lifecycle stage, NetProspex was able to test different content combinations to find the one that best moved their prospects to the next phase of the purchase lifecycle.

It also shows the interactive nature of the Nurture Marketing Classification and Nurture process. Each behavior—positive or negative—exhibited by a prospect altered what NetProspex would do next. Each site visit or engagement with the organization added to their knowledge base for each individual. Persona segments and offerings were continually refined based on the real-time activities of their prospects and their reaction to the past offerings. NetProspex continually managed their Nurture program and let the actions of each prospect determine the next step in the relationship.

Paperstyle

Paperstyle is an organization that has been offering invitations and stationary online since 1999. While the organization offers a wide variety of invitations and stationary for all types of occasions, they wanted to use Nurture Marketing for one of their strongest markets – weddings.

Target Interests

Paperstyle analyzed their customer database and identified that wedding invitations and related products were a high value audience for them. In analyzing that market and the products purchased, they identified two distinct target audiences. There were those who needed products for their own weddings and those who need to purchase invitations and other stationary for a friend or a relative's wedding.

Those individuals planning their own weddings had a unique persona and very distinct purchasing patterns. The same was true of the markets purchasing for another person's wedding. This distinction made wedding planning a perfect situation for a Nurture Marketing program.

Create Relevant

To create relevance, Paperstyle analyzed purchase patterns of these two markets and saw they purchased completely different sets of products and had very specific purchase patterns. For those purchasing items for their own weddings, they first purchased wedding essentials – invitations, RSPVs and other products. They then purchased wedding favors, bridal party gifts and, finally, thank you cards. The key purchase patterns of those planning their own weddings is these purchase events were weeks apart.

For those helping plan another's wedding, the purchase pattern was different both in terms of products purchased and the tempo of these purchases. While those purchasing for their own weddings took weeks between purchases, friend's wedding planners made purchases on a much faster pace. Their purchases of bridal shower products, bachelorette party items, and then wedding gifts occurred within weeks.

To create relevance, Paperstyle designed a Nurture Marketing program designed to the purchase propensities and purchase tempo of each target audience. Their plan was to move the individuals in both markets to their website, separate them using a new webpage developed for the program, and then move them down the product purchase lifecycle as they planned their celebrations.

Go Fishing

To attract them to the site, Paperstyle used email marketing and other acquisition sources to move people to a webpage designed specifically for these two audiences. Because weddings are trigger event markets, they needed to allocate dollars to maintain a constant acquisition effort. The goal was to use social and traditional marketing channels to reach individuals as they became engaged or were asked to be a part of a friend's wedding and move them to the site.

Once at Paperstyle's webpage, the wedding prospect was presented with two options – Your Wedding? Or Friend or Relative's wedding? Depending on which track they selected, they were moved into the appropriate Nurture program.

Classify

Unlike the business to business case presented previously, there was no need to initially classify the Paperstyle wedding prospects. They did it themselves. However, once they clicked on one of the two tracks, Paperstyle began collecting information on both individuals and their purchase needs. While their classification was done by the consumer, they still collected data from this first contact to identify key wedding dates, information about the individual visiting their site and their product needs. This Nurture Program information was housed in a database to be enhanced and analyzed to drive future contacts. A cookie was also placed on the computer system of the individual to track future visits to the organization's site.

Nurture

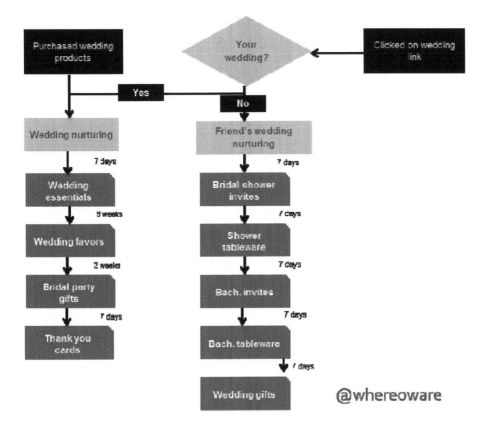

Their Nurture Marketing program identified the likely product purchase cycle of each wedding group. Developed by the organization, Silverpop, and their agency - @whereoware – each track used past purchase tendencies to pace the relationship marketing effort. Silverpop's Nurture Marketing system tracked each purchase to determine the next step in the relationship. While the tracks shown here were the initial ones, they would modify them with each visit the individual made to the organization's site and each response to an emailed effort.

What Were the Results?

One of the benefits of a Nurture Marketing strategy is you can classify the prospects immediately, and if the purchase product sequence is fairly established, you can automate most of the program. That is what Paperstyle accomplished. Their Nurture system was able to adjust based on visitation and email reactions and then plan the next contact for each individual on their Nurture database.

In comparing their Nurture Marketing system with prior performance, Paperstyle had the following results:

- Open rates increased 244%
- Click rate increased 161%
- Revenue per cycle increase 330%

Paperstyle Summary

Paperstyle is now working with Silverpop and @whereoware to develop Nurture Marketing strategies for their Sweet 16, Baby and Anniversary programs. Like all social marketing strategies, the key is to design them for each unique audience you want to develop but roll them out in a controlled fashion. This allows your organization to focus on the unique characteristics of each market to ensure the new strategy will be a success.

7

The Social IMC Marketing Strategy

The Social IMC strategy is diametrically opposed to Engagement Marketing. Engagement Marketing strives to engage anonymously with a broad target market. Social IMC strives to develop a deep, holistic, database-driven relationship with a targeted high-value market. Engagement Marketing wants to increase the organization's social footprint. Social IMC is focused on maximizing market share, helping them achieve their mission, and selling products and services by helping each individual achieve their community goals. Engagement Marketing uses Awesome content to engage its market. Social IMC takes a relationship to the ultimate level by using Empowerment as the base for its marketing strategy.

The ultimate goal of the Social IMC marketing strategy is simple. You want to capture a major share of a market that represents the highest value or highest opportunity for your organization. Done correctly, the Social IMC marketing strategy moves these high-value prospects and customers to a virtual community page or mobile application designed to empower them by helping them address the major challenges that face their virtual communities By focusing on the needs of the community, you create a place where they can safely engage with each other and use the information and content created by your organization.

Why is Social IMC so powerful? First, it moves a high-value market off the social networks to a place where you can control the message. Second, because the Social IMC strategy builds and uses a marketing database from the outset of the relationship, you can use this knowledge to engage with your virtual community members. You can separate customers from prospects, and determine their personas and the products and services they're most likely to purchase. Finally, the Social IMC strategy is powerful because it provides an actual, significant benefit to the virtual community. If your organization helps the community address their challenges, they'll not only remain on your site, they will tell others about it.

Developing and Deploying a Social IMC Strategy

The Social IMC strategy is developed, deployed, and measured in five steps. While its steps look much like those found in the last two strategies, they are is very different. In Social IMC, we are looking to develop a long-term, holistic relationship with the customers and prospects in a high-value target market. To accomplish this goal, we want to create a private virtual community designed to empower the individuals. This virtual community—either on a website or delivered through a mobile app—will link to a database designed to track how the community uses the assets we provide to them. Linked to your sales and marketing systems, you will have a 360° view of all of the community members and their relationship with your organization.

In Social IMC, the enticement to encourage the target market to become a member of your community is the Empowering idea. This is something you create to help the community accomplish their mission. To get to the empowering item, members need to go through an Information Exchange where they create a user ID and password. Each time they return to the community, they need to log in to get to the resources you are providing. They benefit from your empowering content and, because they log-in each time they visit, you get to track, classify, and engage with them.

The following are the five steps required to build a successful Social IMC strategy:

Target Communities

Unlike the other social strategies, the Social IMC strategy is focused on building a virtual community for one of your highest value markets. The goal is to move your highest value prospects away from your competitors and place them on a private virtual community you cre-

ate for them. While we will get to the trick of how to make it so attractive your high-value target market will join, the first task is to identify the target market you want to attract.

In initiating a Social IMC strategy development project, you'll identify, define, and build the persona of your high-value market just like you did in the other two strategies. You'll want to size and value the total markets, identify the percentage that's active on social networks and sites, then determine exactly who they are

In developing your target markets, keep in mind that you'll want your Social IMC strategy to focus on only your highest value or highest opportunity markets. This is because the Social IMC strategy will cost more to maintain a 360° view of each individual's relationship. Because you're identifying and analyzing your highest-value markets, it's often useful to move beyond the free social monitoring systems overviewed earlier and use more sophisticated pay-for-use systems, like Radian6, IBM Digital Analytics, and Netbase.

Pay-for-use social monitoring systems have the following advantages over free systems:

1. Historical view: Free social monitoring systems only report on what is happening now. Pay-for-use systems allow you to examine results historically. This allows you to look at key topics, products, or competitors to identify changes over time.

2. Greater control: Pay-for-use systems allow you to really hone in on your target markets to monitor their social activities. You can examine the social conversation in extreme detail and learn where they're happening in the social media pyramid, and who is at the center of each topic.

3. More capabilities: Pay-for-use systems give you a number of capabilities not available with free systems. They allow you to better identify the influencers at the center of topic discussions, create word clouds used to define topic conversations, and better analyze the size and location of communities relevant to your target market.

With Social IMC you need to deeply understand the social characteristics of the high-value target market you want to develop. If you understand what they're talking about, who the leaders are, the tone and sentiment regarding you and your competitors, and where the conversation is occurring in the social pyramid, you will be positioned to do something exceptional to attract your target market. Using pay-for-use social monitoring systems gives you the insights you'll need.

Create Empowerment

The key to a successful Social IMC program is your ability to empower your high-value target markets. Every trigger event and passion community is on a mission. This mission is their reason for existing. If you can recognize that mission and create a way to empower community members to achieve it, they'll beat a path to your virtual private community. And, if you add other capabilities and resources into the community, you can keep them coming back.

Regardless of whether you're targeting consumers or businesses, you need to undertake a three-step process to create something empowering. Keep in mind empowerment is in the eyes of your target market, so it will be framed from their perspective. These are the three steps you need to develop:

1. **Mission:** Every community is on a mission. It's the reason passion and trigger event communities form in the first place. Sometimes their mission is stated, sometimes it's just known, and other times it's in the aspirations of their members. Remember, it's *not* about your products or services or even about your organization. It's about them and what they're trying to achieve or accomplish. Build a virtual private community to help them and they will happily become a part of it.

2. **Empowering Concept:** Determine what you can do to help them achieve their goals, their dreams, and their mission. You can build tools, give critical information, create an empowering mobile app, or give access and the ability to engage with experts in a unique way. Whatever it is you do, it must be something that truly connects with the mission. You'll get their attention and they'll likely tell others about your empowering concept and the ways you're making it a reality.

3. **Coherent components:** In the Social IMC strategy, your goal is to develop a long-term relationship with your high-value market. This means you not only want them to go to the private virtual community or mobile app you built for them, you want to keep them coming back. Around your empowering content, you might want to add a place for relevant text and video content, forum pages to discuss different topics, live chat or chat rooms to dialog with members, and other features designed to engage members over time. You should also build a great profile page where each member can place information and photos relevant to the community. Coherent

components make the site or app more useful to community members.

In building your empowering concept, always remember empowerment is in the eye of the beholder. When creating your empowering concept, it does not have to be within the expertise of your organization. For example, one client wanted to attract key CEOs within the industry. The CEOs were not interested in talking about the products and services of this organization. They had people to do that. What they wanted was to hear from connected individuals about what was happening with the economy, governmental regulations, and topics like green energy and the environment.

To empower these CEOs, the organization created a series of webinars featuring key business and governmental people who would address specific issues of importance to them. These webinars featured live discussions of important topics and forum discussions afterward. During these webinars, there was no sales discussion whatsoever. The organization was dedicated to empowering the CEOs to help them achieve their mission. However, when it came time to sell these companies, they had an inside track with the CEOs .

Once you have your empowering concept, you'll place it in a private virtual community site. To get to this site, members of your target market will need to go through an information exchange where they give you their e-mail address, create a passwords, and answer key questions to gain admittance. Unlike the Nurture Marketing strategy, you will create a "My Profile" page for each individuals. On these pages, they can update their profile, opt-in and out of your marketing activities, and add photos and other information. In a Social IMC private community site, members often want to share their profiles with other community members.

You'll find if you make the virtual private community a part of your website, potential community members will be suspect of your motivations. A better strategy is to build the community as a separate site with a name relevant to their mission. To show them you're sponsoring the community, put your logo on the bottom with the text, "Powered By." This positions you as a supporter of the community and its mission and, when the time is right, they can click on it to reach you. You can take them to your website, connect them to live chat, or message them to answer their queries.

To keep members coming back, you will want to add new articles and videos relevant to the community mission, develop forum pages so community members can discuss important topics, and develop capabilities to make the private virtual community site vibrant and alive. You want your site to be one community members will use consistently. Your goal is to use the empowering concept to attract them to the site and your additional coherent elements to keep them coming back.

Go Viral

To attract your target market to your private community, you need a Go Viral marketing plan. This plan will utilize every marketing channel used by your target market to engage them and move them to the page containing the information exchange. This then allows them to join the private community you developed.

To drive a large portion of your target market to your new private community site, you need to focus your resources on a short time period. Remember, communities have short attention spans, so initially you want a coordinated marketing program to reach them in all of the marketing channels they tend to use. Keep your marketing program short, focused, multichannel, and multimedia.

The graphic is useful to see the structure of a Go Viral marketing program. The goal is to establish a week or two where you want to focus your marketing efforts. You'll want to coordinate all relevant marketing channels to feature ads, videos, and articles about your new community site. Generally, you'll be featuring your empowering concept and its benefits to the target community.

When building your program, it's useful to separate marketing channels into three types. Long-tail marketing channels are those you need several months to develop. You can start on these while you're developing the empowering element and support community. Your goal is to schedule the ads and articles to run during the weeks where you will be announcing your new virtual private community.

Medium-tail channels can be developed more rapidly. These channels include banner advertising, e-mail communications, Facebook and other social ads, and sponsored videos you will place on YouTube, Vimeo, and other video sites. Because these channels are more flexible compared to the long-tailed channels, you can develop suites of banner ads or multiple articles and e-mails to communicate with your target markets. During the several weeks when you are promoting your new virtual community site, you can deliver multiple messages using these channels.

Short-tail channels are those where you can deliver multiple messages to your target audience each day or every other day. They're highly flexible, allowing you to send out different messages throughout the day to see which one is the best to reach your target market. Short-tail channels containing relevant communities—LinkedIn, Google+, and Twitter—can even be used to carry on conversations with community members about your empowering content or tool. If your offering is of interest to them they will engage in daily conversation.

To manage your Go Viral program, it's useful to create a master calendar for each channel you'll use. Develop separate timelines to test and broadcast each message. For highly flexible channels, develop specific messages you want to communicate within each channel. Also identify the key hash tags to reach people discussing specific topics on Twitter. For the short-tail channels, create many messages to discuss the multiple topics related to your community offering.

Influential bloggers are critical to the success of your Go Viral marketing program. They reach directly into the community you want to attract to your site and often speak to a significant share of the total market. To get them excited about your community offering, talk to them about your empowering concept to make sure it will excite and engage community members. Remember, they want to be viewed as an insider in the community. You may want to consider giving them some time prior to your announcement of the new site and empowering concept to tell their readership. Essentially, let them scoop the marketplace. This will give them the prestige they are seeking within the community while communicating to your target market your community support. This creates a win-win situation for you and them.

Identify

The identification step in the Social IMC strategy is much like the nurture step in Nurture Marketing. The Nurture Marketing strategy uses a landing page to gather and database information about the visitor and then sends them permission to get the relevant content. Social IMC

takes them to the home page of the virtual community site. They can see some information but, to receive all of the benefits, they must register. In both processes, you want to gather log in information, ask key questions to initially categorize the individual, and any opt-in information related to the community and your efforts to support it.

Like the Nurture Marketing strategy, the information in the database can be augmented with descriptive business or consumer data. In addition, it can be matched to your sales and marketing systems to learn if the community member is a customer or a prospect. From this information, you can then begin establishing the persona of each individual in your community.

Social IMC differs from Nurture Marketing in how the data is used. In Nurture Marketing, your goal is to drive e-mail messages to move the individual through the product purchase lifecycle toward a fast sale. You add a cookie to their computer then use this link to develop a more complete persona.

In Social IMC, you have a different relationship with the community member. Every time they engage with you, they must log into the site which gives you an instant link to your database. With this link, you can determine their interests and involvement in the community to develop new relevant content. You goal is to support the community and then be there when they're ready to purchase.

Engage

From your monitoring of community members, you learn what they need to accomplish their community mission. Use these insights to post new content to keep your virtual community vibrant and up-to-date. You don't need to interact directly with the community members, but moni-

tor the forum to make sure there are no trolls or bullies. If there are, get rid of them. Your role in the community should be transparent and supportive.

While you ultimately want to sell your products and services, don't sell directly. Just offer them a way to engage once they are ready to move forward. When an individual is ready to purchase they can reach you by clicking on your "Powered by (Your Name)" log at the bottom of the page. Remember, months or years of using your private community site to accomplish their community's mission keeps your organization positioned when they are ready to purchase.

How Do You Position Your Products in a Social IMC Program?

This is the question most frequently asked by CMOs when discussing their Social IMC strategy. From our experience, there are three ways you can position your products in a Social IMC solution:

Your Product as an Enabler: One way is to make the purchase of your product a requirement for the targeted prospect to gain admission to the empowering community. For example, in the next chapter we'll see a brewing organization that requires you to purchase a beer to obtain a code contained in the beer cap. Once you have the code, you can use it to get to the information exchange and then to the community. The purchase of the beer enabled your access to the community.

If your product purchase is low and the community you're targeting is enraptured with your empowering tool or site, they may be willing to make a purchase to gain access to the community. However, this is not for most companies. If you want to make your product an enabler, check it out with current customers in the target market and/ or influential bloggers to see if this is acceptable to them. For some products, it will not be. For package goods and other impulse products, it might be a way to ensure product sales from your Social IMC communities.

Your Product as an Enhancer: A second option is to make your product an enhancer of the relationship between a community member and you. Some companies use a product purchase to give the community member more power or status within the community. They don't have to purchase, but, if they do, they'll receive more than community members who don't.

Your Product as an Extra: This is the most common relationship between your products and services and a virtual community. At the bottom of every page on your site or on the profile page in a mobile app, you'll show the community is "Powered by" your organization. You can have the statement and your logo there. If the individual clicks on the logo, they will be taken to a site where you can talk about your organization. Include a live-chat feature, information about the organization's products and services, frequently asked questions (FAQ) and other features. If they go to this level, they're ready to engage with you. Out in the community, you are an expert. Here, you are a marketer trying to position your organization and your products to meet their needs.

The key to success is to place your products and services in a place that will not disrupt the relationship. Do this and the community will work effectively. Then, when they have a need, they can initiate the move from community member to prospect. Your goal is to *be there* when they are ready to purchase. And, if your site is effective in enabling them, you will have removed them from the sight of your competitors and make it easy for them to purchase from you when they're ready.

Social IMC Results Metrics

The Social IMC strategy is designed to develop a long-term relationship with customers and prospects in a specific high-value target market. From the very first engagement, the strategy builds a database that can be enhanced and used to define, classify and measure every part of their relationship with your organization. Because they log in each time they come to the virtual community, you can precisely measure every investment you made to communicate with the individual, and the revenue generated from having the relationship. You have total tracking of the relationship and, as a result, can determine the profitability of the program from the individual, from a persona segment, or from the total Social IMC effort.

Beyond that, remember you will be matching your private virtual community members with the information on your sales and marketing system. You can also enhance each record with business or consumer descriptive overlay data. Unlike any other strategy, Social IMC does give you a true 360° view of the individual. You'll know every interaction you have had with them—regardless of the marketing channel—and track every response to these stimuli. You'll be able to accurately measure your investment in each person, and the individual and aggregate purchases they are and will make.

Because Social IMC connects your social efforts to final results, you can establish KPIs and track them throughout the individual's relationship with your organization. As we will explore in chapter nine, we can establish a relationship funnel from the total segment through to the first and subsequent sales. Because the funnel will list every step in the relationship process, we can use it to establish the KPIs we need to track at every step for success. It gives us the goals and constant metrics we need to succeed. We can then use our social/web tracking systems like the IBM digital suite, Adobe Omniture system or even Google Analytics to monitor funnel performance and identify the efficient and inefficient elements of our Social IMC plan. You can test alternatives for the inefficient elements to learn the best ways to engage, empower, and acquire your high value markets.

Social IMC truly matches your social investment with the other sales and marketing efforts you're executing. Because it tracks the relationship from initial contact through to all purchases, it gives your organization the KPIs needed to track every step in the relationship development process. This will help you justify and manage your Social IMC program.

Strategy Limitations

There are several limitations you need to consider in developing and deploying a Social IMC strategy. The first is the investment required to develop one. Social IMC needs to have a database and secure entry system, empowering content to attract new members, highly relevant content to keep them current, and a commitment from the organization to maintain it over time. For this reason, the Social IMC strategy should be reserved for your highest value markets. Your goal is to remove them from open social networking systems and take them to a secure, interesting, and relevant site where they can engage with other, like-minded, community members. This strategy allows you to engage with them in a virtual community where you can best position your organization and your brands while focusing on the specific needs of your target market. The database and the fact that they must log in to get to the community makes it a costly but totally database-driven community site. A major investment that will produce major returns in your highest-value markets.

In addition to its cost, the other limitation to a Social IMC strategy is its intense focus on the community. While this is what gives the strategy its strength, it also means your organization must commit the resources to become a central part of each Social IMC community. This is resource intensive but really pays off, as you will see in the next section. Social IMC is a commitment between your organization and the targeted virtual community. Make the commitment in the markets where the return for your investment will be high.

Best Applications

Remember, this is for your high-value markets. Your strategy is to remove them from your competitors so you can build a strong, knowledge-based relationship with them. Done right, it's a powerful and highly engaging strategy. The goal—to a degree—is to forget your organization and learn the needs and motivations of the high-value communities you want to build. Truly understand their mission and their motivations, and you'll transcend being an organization to become a leader and guide as they address their community missions. For your highest value markets, isolating them in a virtual, empowering community is the best way to grow your market share in your most profitable markets.

Social IMC Summary

Social IMC is designed to empower a market on a private community site designed expressly for them. Your goal is to meet their needs by addressing the mission of the community. By building tools, forums, and other support capabilities you become a core part of their community. Giving them special webinars, chats, and other networking/

social capabilities establishes your expertise and your willingness to help the community achieve its mission.

Social IMC is the strongest relationship an organization can develop with a community. It takes your highest-value markets into a private exchange that you control—meaning no competitors. You can then help the community with engaging content, keep members coming back with empowering tools, and integrate your products and services to be there when they're ready to purchase. It's the social strategy with the most control, most trackability, and most impact on the markets of highest value to your organization.

8

Social IMC Case Studies

The case study chapters are designed to use videos and images to show you the components and results from each case example. While we have included links in this book, occasionally YouTube, Vimeo and other links will fail. If you cannot get them to open, you can find working copies, as well as newer case examples, on the book's website at www.SocialIMC.com.

Social IMC strategies are unique in that they use the mission of the community to build a link between a high-value target market and the organization. In this chapter, you'll see a broad range of business and consumer focused Social IMC programs. In addition, we have selected several international programs to show you that you can deploy a Social IMC strategy in any country.

Note: All of the examples in this chapter have been developed from YouTube and Vimeo videos produced by that organization or their advertising agencies. Analysis was also developed from examination of articles featuring organization executives or advertising managers on the campaigns used here.

ONE.org Agit8

Started by Bono, the lead singer of the band U2, ONE.org is dedicated to ending poverty in Africa. While it is a Not-for-Profit organization, it does not develop its following like traditional Not-for-Profit organizations. In a traditional NFP, people are asked to donate their time and/or dollars to help the cause. To grow, the NFP must continually market to their donor base to get the resources necessary to continue operations to achieve their group's goals.

ONE.org is different. They don't ask for your money to achieve their goals. They ask for your voice. ONE.org's method is to mobilize involved citizens to approach governments and organizations throughout the world with petitions, letters, phone calls, and in person visits requesting specific actions be taken to end extreme poverty and preventable disease in Africa. Initially, ONE.org will ask you to join their organization by providing your e-mail on a petition they're developing to help their cause. They then ask you to "Amplify your Voice" by sending postcards to your Congressional representatives, visiting their offices, or doing other activities to let them know you support the mission and the causes of ONE.org.

While ONE.org has been extremely successful in growing their organization and helping begin the process of eradicating poverty in Africa, they wanted to reach new markets. Ideally, they wanted to attract new members who would not only sign petitions but would amplify their voices by virally activating their friends to become advocates—in person or electronically—to help the organization achieve its mission. The Agit8 (pronounced like *agitate*) Social IMC program is an example of their efforts to grow into these new markets.

Target Communities

While ONE.org was actively growing, they wanted to better penetrate the millennial and boomer populations. Specifically, they wanted to appeal to individuals who loved music and identified with activists who had changed the world at concerts like Live Aid and Live8. They knew these individuals would be attracted to the message of ONE.org but they needed a way to reach them and bring them into the ONE membership. To accomplish this, they created the Agit8 program.

They knew their target market was people who loved music and who recognized its ability to change the world. If they selected the right songs and the right artists, ONE.org felt they would reach the intended audience. Their goal was to significantly grow their market awareness and market share in these key millennial and boomer markets and motivate them to become more active in the causes of ONE.org.

Create Empowerment

If ONE.org simply approached their markets talking about extreme poverty and foreign aid, it would have been much more difficult to reach key markets and garner as many actions. These markets were not (yet) activated to their causes. However, they were music lovers who responded to the messages that folk and activist songs contained. They related to the music, the artists, and the messages of the songs. To reach their markets, ONE.org needed to use music as a tool to reach, engage, and activate this important new market.

ONE.org Agit8
Program Video 2013

However, music was not the whole answer. Millennials did not know many of the original artists who were big in the '60s, '70s, and even the '80s. To address this challenge, ONE.org talked to a wide range of diverse artists and asked them to participate in their program by singing protest songs of the past and present. They knew these songs hit a chord with their target markets and, by having newer artists sing them, they would in turn attract each artist's market. They used OPN, Other People's Networks, to increase awareness and market share.

If you take a look at even a partial list of artists you can see their musical diversity. Bruce Springsteen, U2, Ed Sheeran, Kid Rock, One Direction, Macklemore and Ryan Lewis, Elvis Costello, and Jessie J were but a few of the artists who agreed to participate in the Agit8 program. ONE.org paired each artist with a protest song. They then created concerts, video performances, interviews, and other content in Africa, Germany, the UK, France, Belgium and the US designed to attract their target global audience.

For the artists, their songs were released on multiple platforms to maximize the impact in their fan markets. You can see some of the artist videos by clicking on the Agit8 icon or by copying this browser link: http://www.youtube.com/watch?v=K8UjZczqJ7I&feature=share &list=PLbpi6ZahtOH4wdTN7RGXsEQvPzEUjN93I. Viewers could join the Agit8 channel on YouTube and, with every video they watched, they were encouraged to join the cause of ONE.org. You will see these activation appeals at the end of every video. To show you the power of this program, as of this writing, there were 18,842,345 people who had joined the program.

Go Viral

In the words of Jeff Davidoff, CMO of ONE.org, the goal of the Agit8 program was to "make content that appears where the market already exists." In his words, ONE.org wanted to "break out of the digital 'Do Gooder' ghetto on social sites and make it to the front page." To accomplish this goal, they used the star power of major artists in the genres which appealed to their target markets. Their marketing plan was to use every available angle to create awareness for the program and ONE.org.

To promote the Agit8 program, ONE.org hosted live concerts, starting with one at the Tate Modern Museum of Art in the UK, the host country for the upcoming G8 Conference. The concert produced 20 – 30 videos that were placed on YouTube and other video channels. For each protest song, ONE.org released the newer artist's version, and they produced the original album lyrics and original art for their fans to view and share. They used Spotify to stream five albums of original and new music that received over 2.3 million streams.

ONE.org used Twitter, YouTube, and Facebook to promote and share content and created their special Agit8 website to create a sense of community with their new fans (http://www.one.org/protestsongs/). In selecting their artists, one of the most effective promotional elements was ONE.org's selection of major YouTube artists to participate in the concerts and recordings. Many of these artists had millions of YouTube followers who already loved their songs. When these individuals were asked to participate in the Agit8 program, their loyal fans followed them to Agit8 and thus to ONE. ONE.org received a huge boost in its Facebook and ONE.org enrollment base, while at the same time these YouTube artists became associated with some of the most famous artists in music today. (Click here to watch Christina Grimme – a YouTube artist playing Aretha Franklin's Respect along with an appeal to help her get enough votes to get this song on the Agit8 album. Getting votes engaged her followers in the Agit8 program[27])

The Agit8 program created a major buzz in the music industry. Numerous articles were written in music magazines like Rolling Stone[28] and other industry news publications, reaching over a billion media impressions. Involved artists appeared for interviews on television and in print, and new organizations talked about upcoming concerts and the goals of the Agit8 program.

Finally, ONE.org used Facebook Ads and search terms on YouTube to attract new participants at a low cost. They also provided the involved artists with content to place on their webpages. What they found was that when the artists added new content to their Facebook and fan pages, their fans who followed them were notified by e-mail of the new content. This produced huge activity on the artist's fan page, which, in turn, brought them to the Agit8 program. It was a great use of OPN –Other People's Networks – to drive the Social IMC program of ONE.org.

Identify

Every Agit8 video, website, and communication encouraged partici-pants to "Amplify their Voice" by becoming a member of ONE.org. To do that, the participant needed to provide ONE.org with their e-mail and other information to become a part of the organization. With the e-mail address, ONE.org could engage in a two-way conversation with its members to ask them to add their voice to different actions in the fight against extreme poverty. With location information, ONE.org could ask its members to go beyond signing petitions to get more di-rect with key legislators in their voting districts. The more engaged the individual, the greater their value to the causes supported by ONE.org.

Engage

To engage their Agit8 members, ONE.org released a continuous stream of new videos from different artists. They also held contests to determine which songs and artists to include on their albums. These albums were important because they were featured on Spotify and other outlets. Getting on an album was important to the artist and many—like Christina Grimme—used their YouTube base to vote them onto the albums.

The stream of content and messages from Agit8 and ONE.org kept its participants involved. In the words of Jeff Davidoff, CMO of ONE.org, their goal was to "keep the content where the people are and to keep them active." ONE.org monitored page views and enroll-ment actions to determine the best artists and protest songs to please their musical audience. They built on the best to continually grow the program.

What Were the Results?

Over the course of the initial Agit8 program, ONE.org received over a billion media impressions. Their program was discussed in *Rolling Stone*, *Spin*, on *Entertainment Tonight*, and other media outlets. Agit8 exposed the organization to a new and valuable market while giving them a listening experience relevant to their worldviews. It combined music and activism in a way the audience found appealing and stimulating.

The videos initially had over seven million views (still growing at 30,000 views a day) which produced over 600,000 actions for ONE. org and Agit8. During the initial program, ONE.org added over 350,000 Facebook fans and over 250,000 new ONE members. These new members became active immediately and have continued to support the efforts of ONE.org.

ONE.org Agit8 Summary

The Agit8 program is a great example of designing, developing, and deploying a Social IMC strategy. The organization identified a new market they wanted to develop and realized they needed to relate to that market in a way that appealed to them. Rather than talk about their causes, they promoted music and artists—but not any music. It was music which was related to the ONE.org mission that also appealed to the target market. It was music but with a purpose.

To develop the program and get it to go viral, ONE.org was an expert in using Other People's Networks. By involving a mix of established big name artists, new emerging stars, and popular YouTube artists, ONE.org was able to use their networks to create viral activity about the program. Jeff Davidoff stated, "One of the biggest surprises was the large audiences many of the YouTube artists brought to the Agit8 program. Many had several million followers who became more engaged with Agit8 and ONE.org activities." In your Social IMC and other strategies, remember the power OPN brings to your program.

People are eager to support their passions and to address their trigger event needs. When they find something they like and support, they'll tell their friends and associates. It's free publicity that will drive your Social IMC strategies to reach the markets you want to develop. OPN is a powerful social tool you can use to drive your programs to new heights.

Carling Black Label—South Africa

Empowering your target community is central to a successful Social IMC strategy. Understanding their needs and then giving them the tools and resources to meet these needs will uniquely position you in their minds. Maintain the positioning and they will keep coming to your virtual community for years. For this example, we look at an organization whose program is in its second year and growing.

Carling Black Label's Social IMC program is strong for three reasons. First, it shows a Social IMC program can exist anywhere in the world. Social IMC is international, and this shows its implementation in South Africa. During a recent talk for Social Media Week (Chicago 2013), a participant asked if it was possible to do social marketing in Africa, where computers are relatively rare. The answer we gave was that while there might not be computers, there are phones - both basic and smart – and the populations of most African nations are relatively connection savvy. Social IMC is not just for developed nations anymore.

A second reason this is an interesting and educational case is because it's a great example of using a mobile application to drive a Social IMC strategy. The goal of Social IMC is to empower the community, place the empowerment in a place where they must exchange information with you, and then give them the resources to address their needs. All of these elements can be achieved with a mobile app. Too often, CEOs and CMOs view social from a networking and website-centric perspective. This is one of a great number of examples of Social IMC that blasts through this perception.

To get a mobile application, the user must register with the organization. This creates a database of the individual. The mobile app can then create a profile for the user. This allows the organization to learn more about the individual while allowing them to become known to the virtual community. Because they identify the user with each visit, mobile applications give the organization the same control as a web-based social marketing program. Further, you can have both a mobile app and a social site, with both requiring registration. This allows your organization to track the community member regardless of the media they use to access their virtual community.

Finally this case is one of the best examples of empowering the community member. It shows the power of Social IMC and how it positions the organization uniquely in the target marketplace. It hit a home run and continues to deliver a high level of engagement in their target market.

Target Communities

Sports fanatics are a unique breed. They're individuals who are knowledgeable about the teams they support and the leagues in which they play. They have strong opinions about their teams, coaches and chances of success, and love to talk about them with other fans. Whether it's an argument about whose team is best or a discussion with others who support their team, sports fans are often seeking other fans to talk with.

Not only do they talk about their favorite teams and sports, many want to show others their coaching skills. In the US, there are fantasy football, baseball, and other sport leagues where fans can select their teams and play other fans in weekly games. In these fantasy leagues, a fan can win money or just recognition when their fantasy team wins.

It shows they know how to pick the players and build a team that can win.

In South Africa, Carling Black Label identified sports fans—specifically fans of football (soccer in the United States). These fans were likely to consume more beer than other market segments, and associated drinking with the sport and the team they loved. They were a passion market with new fans joining every year. And they were loyal to their teams, their fellow fans, and the drinks they loved to consume while their sport was being played. For Carling Black Label, the football sports fan represented a high-value market they wanted to engage and develop. If the organization could link its beer to their passions for football, they would have loyal beer drinking fans for generations.

Create Engagement

Think about any passionate sports fan you know and the way they relate to their team. If they lose, they criticize the team for calling the wrong play, poorly managing the situation, or having too little talent. If they win, they cheer but also identify places where the team could have improved.

For these fans, their fantasy aspiration would be to *be the coach*. If they could control the team, they could do it better than the current coaches. So that is what Carling Black Label and their agency, Ogilvy South Africa, set out to accomplish. They wanted to find a way for the sports fans in South Africa to be the coach.

To achieve this empowering concept, Carling Black Label got the two top professional teams—the Kaiser Chiefs and the Orlando Pirates—to agree to a single game called the Carling Black Label Cup. It would be a major match, held in a large stadium, and would award money and a cup to the winner. It would decide which one of these teams was the best for that year.

To enable the fans, Carling Black Label created a mobile app and a number of supporting sites. The app was designed to let each fan declare which team they supported. Once they downloaded the app, they could use it to determine the starters on their team. The votes would be counted and the starters declared for the game. The fans, not the coaches, would determine who would start in the game.

To get the access to the contest with the app, the fan had to purchase Carling Black Label beer which had a code printed under the cap. (Whether they drank the beer is unclear, but I am betting they did!) There could only be one fan per code. The fan had to purchase a beer to get access to the contest. This meant the product was the enabler.

According to Ogilvy, the mobile app was a single tool that allowed the participant to learn about each player, review the current state of the voting, and allow the fans to debate their selections. Coaches could also talk about their teams using Twitter and Facebook. The mobile site was easy to use and worked on any web-enabled mobile phone.[29]

Go Viral

The first Carling Black Label Cup was in 2011. To announce it, they featured Ruud Guilt—a well know coach—telling about the cup and the fan's role in it (http://youtu.be/d4YtsEXS-mY). The marketing communications talked directly to the fans, and the fact they would be empowered to "Be the Coach." They used social, sports print media, television, and radio to get the word out. The ads were run on video sites like YouTube and Vimeo. Once the fans learned of the campaign, it quickly went viral and grew the program to historic levels.

Carling Black Label South Africa
Be The Coach link http://youtu.be/d4YtsEXS-mY

Identify

When the fans registered to get their app, they created a database of their activities and a way for Carling Black Label to maintain contact with them. Upon registration, the organization knew the team the individual was supporting and the players they wanted to start in the match. They also knew the amount of time and the number of visits.

Throughout the lead up to the cup game, as well as during and after it, Carling Black Label communicated with the fans supporting both teams to tell them the status of their players. They targeted them with updates and information to keep each fan current on the effectiveness of their coaching job. Fans could also access the site to see up-to-the-minute results. The fans loved the two-way communication because it was about a topic they were deeply interested and invested in. Carling Black Label was just powering the event and making their dreams of coaching come true.

Engage

The app and the program did not stop with the start of the game. During the game, they could SMS their coaching staff with who should be substituted (SMS stands for Short Message Service and is the text message you send and receive with your mobile phone.) It allowed the fans to control the game as it actually progressed. Find the "Live Substitution" video at http://youtu.be/SO-gnAL2KBQ or click on Ruud's picture.

What Were the Results?

By every metric, this empowering Social IMC program was a success. In seven weeks there were more than 10.5 million votes cast by the fans. The organization's Facebook site grew by over 450 percent and their Twitter site grew by 600 percent. During the seven weeks of the program, sports sites and sports commentators generated an estimate $7.6 million dollars in free publicity about the game, the fan's selections, and the Carling Black Label program. The event was sold out and millions watched the game from home. To see more about the program, click on the icon or watch it on the Ogilvy agency site. (http://www.ogilvy.co.za/2011/11/carling-black-label-be-the-coach-case-study/)

Carling Black Label South Africa
Ogilvy Case Study link
http://www.ogilvy.co.za/2011/11/carling-black-label-be-the-coach-case-study/

Carling Black Label South Africa Summary

Today, Carling Black Label is starting its third year of their cup series. One of the advantages of developing a virtual, private relationship with your high-value market is you can maintain the relationship over a period of years. With each new year, Carling Black Label can quickly contact last year's participants and get them involved in this year's voting. They offer them daily prizes, game tickets, and other enticements to keep the relationship active. Because the entire contest is focused on the aspirational mission of their members, they quickly become involved and tell their fan friends to become involved as well. Each year builds on the relationship rather than trying to acquire the same market year after year.

Carling Black Label's "Be the Coach" is a best-of-breed example of the Social IMC strategy at work. It targets a high-value market with a mobile app that empowers fans to achieve their wildest dream—to coach their team. It's designed to keep fans involved while building a strong, database driven relationship with them for the long term. It is Social IMC in action.

North Face—China

North Face had a real challenge. They wanted to enter the market in China. The challenge was the markets they wanted to engage did not aspire to be explorers, or to look like one. They had little or no knowledge of North Face, its products, or its brand positioning.

North Face wanted to develop a Social IMC type program to accomplish three goals. They wanted to target a high-value market in China to:

1) Introduce them to North Face and its brand in a way that would let them live the brand.
2) Show examples of North Face products of interest to their target market.
3) Establish North Face as a brand doing business in China.

They wanted a program that would not only achieve these strategic objectives but one that could be tracked to the final purchase. They wanted to know that it produced bottom-line profits for the organization. The program had to link the Social IMC program to the organization's sales and marketing systems to show that involved individuals later purchased North Face products. Like the previous Social IMC program, this one had ROI as well. The difference is they published their results for you to see.

Target Communities

The high-value market North Face wanted to target was young, urban Chinese. These men and women had the discretionary spending capability but were unaware of North Face and The challenge was the target market was not only unaware of North Face but, worse, had little understanding of the brand and its positioning in the marketplace. North Face represented a lifestyle which was unfamiliar to the target market. Adventurism and conquering new places was not a part of the aspirations of the young Chinese North Face wanted to engage and acquire. The organization needed a strategy to engage this high-value market in a way they would better understand North Face and its clothing lines.

Create Empowerment

North Face needed a marketing concept that would demonstrate its brand essence to this target market and allow them to see and purchase North Face products. Rather than try a traditional approach, they decided to have Ogilvy Shanghai create an empowering concept using Social IMC and mobile marketing.

North Face uses the term "Never Stop Exploring" as its brand essence. North Face and Ogilvy Shanghai developed a contest that embraced this and the power of exploration. The goal of the contest was to show the individual the fun of exploration. They used the idea of planting a flag when you conquered a site as the action signifying exploration and North Face.

Individuals could find a location they wanted to conquer. Using their mobile phones, they would plant a virtual flag into the ground. The phone's geo-location system would then transmit to the North Face database the location of the flag, the name the individual assigned the location, and the ID of the individual. This made their conquest official.

The goal was to allow individuals to participate in a unique experience and compete with others to claim China. When visiting the website, they could also see North Face clothing and other products designed for the urban explorer.

Go Viral

The Go Viral program of Ogilvy and North Face was a combination of traditional and social marketing in an integrated effort. The organization used traditional advertising—TV, e-mail, and print—to complement its online marketing effort. In addition, North Face advertised on mobile, in stores, and using field marketing. They also held live events both before and during the contest.

Large screens located on the sides of buildings allowed urban dwellers to see a live, real-time tally showing the number and location of claimed areas within China. This enhanced the gaming aspect of the program and moved people to get involved in the contest. The Go Viral plan, like the contest itself, was a focused, highly concentrated effort to generate maximum buzz to create maximum impact within the target market.

Identify

Through their database, North Face was able to track the activities of the participants. They were also able to link participants to their sales and marketing systems. This allowed them to track not only their activities in the program but their purchase behaviors during and after the contest concluded. It gave Northface a 360° view of the prospects and customers generated through the program.

In addition, North Face was also able to have a two-way conversation with the contest participants. They were able to promote their on-ground rallies, show the leaders with the most flag plantings as well as link the participants to the North Face stores—both virtual and real. The program generated new, young, urban prospects North Face could build into loyal customers.

Engage

During the event, participants and others could watch it unfold in real-time on the event website, through the North Face website, and using the mobile monitors. Periodic live events in major Chinese cities further hyped the event and maintained interest. Combined with in-store retail promotions and field events and promotions, North Face and Ogilvy kept their target market interested and growing throughout the competition.

The program yielded a database North Face could use to continue to build a relationship with the program participants. It created a two-way communication channel between the organization and the participants. It gave them a fun way to learn about North Face and what it represents. It was a great example of linking an organization, its brand positioning, and its products with the exact target market it wanted to develop.

What Were the Results?

The North Face – China Case 2011
Link http://youtu.be/6ktKwssCH-Y

Did it work? You can watch the results and a great overview of the entire program by viewing Ogilvy's video called North Face Red Flags (http://youtu.be/6ktKwssCH-Y). The event involved over 2.2 million Chinese with 651,000 red flags actually planted during the eighteen-day event. The champion of the contest planted over four thousand flags! Because the Social IMC program could link to the North Face sales and marketing systems, North Face noted an increase of over 106 percent in sales during the contest period. In addition, when the final results were tallied, the Social IMC type effort produced a 306 percent return over budget. The result was highly profitable for North Face.

Beyond the event, North Face now has a mobile app and link to these high-value customers and prospects that they can now differentiate on their database. They have key behavioral information on both the event and their use of the North Face website and purchases at retail locations. The Social IMC program formed a link with these individuals that can be developed and nurtured by North Face in the future. It was a great entrance into China that paid immediate benefits and positioned North Face as the adventurous brand of clothing in China. A major accomplishment for a great brand.

North Face Summary

Often, when we think about developing a social strategy, we focus on existing markets. North Face shows you can use Social IMC strategies to impact high opportunity markets. These are markets with relatively low awareness of your organization but with a high potential if you can penetrate them.

Virtual communities are open to any individual or organization that can assist them in achieving their mission. Give them a reason to participate that resonates with them and the tools to make it fun and successful and they will bring themselves and their friends to join your virtual community. Gamify it by awarding them with power, access, status or stuff and you'll have a Social IMC program they will find highly engaging for the long term. North Face used these strategic elements in their Red Flags program with great effect.

Finally, North Face is a great example of how a Social IMC strategy can link to the organization's bottom line. While the examples in this chapter had the same type of metrics, North Face provided actual ROI calculations. All Social IMC programs are designed to link the social program to your sales and marketing systems. As a result, you can track each individual, each unique persona segment and each source through to their purchases with your organization. As a result, your social investment is linked to the revenues which drive your business. As the North Face example shows, it moves social from an unmeasurable risk to a trackable, database driven program with bottom-line implications. It's a well-done program.

9

Justifying Your Social Marketing Program

To justify your social investment, you need to establish key success metrics to show senior management your social investment will payoff for the organization. To create a presentation you can use, there are four steps you need to take. Each is designed to systematically give you the information and graphics you will need to show this justification.

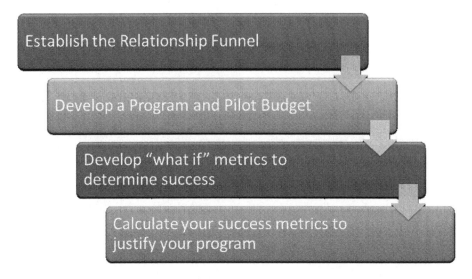

Establish the Relationship Funnel

Develop a Program and Pilot Budget

Develop "what if" metrics to determine success

Calculate your success metrics to justify your program

Step 1: Establish the Relationship Funnel

A relationship funnel is designed to show the steps an individual or business must move through to become a customer. It starts with the total target market and moves, step-by-step, through to the initial purchase (or beyond). You need to show every step the individual takes before they make their first purchase.

- Total Target Market
- Total Social Market
- Info Exchange Landing Page
- Registration Accepted
- Website / Mobile Use
- Product Inquiry
- First Purchase
- Best Customer

The relationship funnel provides you with much more than a visualization of the sales process. It gives you a structured approach to build your organization's success metrics for your social programs. As you quantify each step, the resulting percentages become your success KPIs. As you roll out your program, you will want to monitor the performance of these key steps daily to ensure they are meeting your expectations. If not, you need to test new ideas to improve performance.

It also gives you a base on which to compare the market potential with the investment (budget) are you requesting the organization to make. The relationship funnel gives you a way to show senior management how you developed your justification numbers. You can then measure actual performance against the plan, make adjustments, and show progress to senior management. Done correctly, the relationship funnel provides you a very useful tool to sell and manage the programs that comprise your social strategy.

Regardless of which of the social strategies you select, the top two steps of the relationship funnel are always the same. The first step is a quantification and valuation of the total target market you want to impact. As we covered in earlier chapters, the total market size can be determined using secondary research sources or online databases from companies like InfoUSA. For most markets, it is relatively simple to develop a fairly accurate quantification number.

In addition to getting a count of the number of people in the total target market, you should calculate the total potential value they represent. This is done by multiplying the total number of people or businesses in the total market by the average first purchase revenue they generate. Why generate a total potential dollar figure? You're going to be selling senior management on investing dollars in your social strategy. It helps to show them the relationship of your investment to the total potential revenue the target market might generate. We have found justifying a $100,000 social strategy is somewhat easier when senior management knows it is going to start to impact a target market valued at $1,000,000,000. It gives your justification better perspective if viewed against potential revenues for the organization.

The next step is determining the total number of people in the social market. This need not be an exact number but a fairly educated guess. In the past, the percentage in social space during the course of a year varied by the age and income of the target market. Today, this is less of an issue. Almost all age bands and income levels use social today. The infusion of both networked and smart mobile phones has leveled the playing field. However, we still recommend you show that 95 percent or some reasonable number of the total market is in the social cloud and the value that segment represents. Never use 100 percent, as no market is totally in social, but, regardless of the geography, most markets have a significant number of members who can be reached using social strategies.

After these two steps, the relationship funnel differs depending on which of the social strategies you're deploying. For Engagement Marketing, you will be deploying a Go Social strategy to attract them to your video or Facebook type networking sites. Therefore, your social networking site is the next stage in the relationship funnel. For the other two strategies, the next relationship funnel step is to attract them to the landing page where they can consider registering for the product.

The funnels are unique. Just keep in mind they represent the steps the individual will take as they move forward to becoming your customer. In developing your relationship funnel, you need to be complete and show all of the steps—even if they are relatively unimportant. Each step must be successfully taken for your strategy to be a success.

While it doesn't look like much now, the relationship funnel is the focal point from which you will develop your senior management justification. You'll use the funnel steps to develop key metrics to not only justify your program but evaluate performance on a day by day basis. In addition, the top to bottom measures will be central to building the key measures senior management measures will use to determine if your social strategies deserve funding. At the end, the relationship funnel will be the way you'll show senior management the benefits your social efforts will bring to the organization.

Step 2: Develop a Program and Pilot Budget

The second step in the justification process is to build the program budget. Regardless of which strategy you are employing, you'll need to invest dollars to produce the desired results. This second step in the process will focus on identifying those investment dollars.

At the start of a new social program, you'll need to make a series of one-time investments to make it happen. You will need to invest in the creation of your social website or mobile app, and your tracking database system, and build any tools or capabilities you'll need to make the site attractive to your target market. While you will use these investments across a number of years as you grow your social program, the investment will impact you in year one.

In many budgets, you would amortize these investments across multiple years. In this discussion, you will place all of the investment costs in year one. This makes for a simpler discussion of the justification process. If you or your CFO wants to distribute costs differently, it's a minor change to this presentation. However, in this discussion, simpler is clearer and just as relevant.

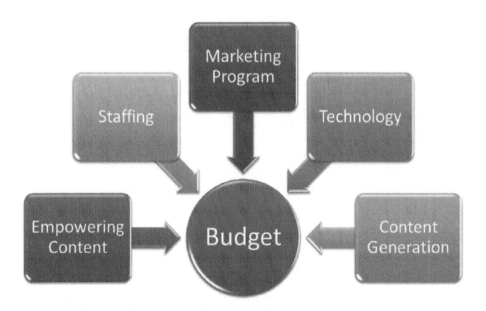

In building your budget, there are five areas you need to quantify:
- Empowering Content: These are the costs to create the content that will attract the prospect to your program.

- Staffing: This is the cost of the marketing team who will manage your program. It includes senior managers and support staff.
- Marketing Program: This is the cost of the elements in your Go Viral or Go Social type marketing programs. It includes all of the channels you anticipate using to engage and attract your markets.
- Technology: This is an aggregate of several cost components. First, two of the three social strategies require a linked database and, often, overlayed descriptive data. Second, there is a cost to develop a virtual private community website and components like blogs, forum pages, live chat, and other required/ desired elements. Third is the cost to develop the mobile apps or required tools for your community. Finally, technology includes the people costs to maintain the site for a year.
- Content Generation: This is a catch-all that includes any costs to maintain the site beyond the empowering component. It's the cost to generate or get new text and video content for the site, the costs to run webinars and other activities, and any extra costs required to make the community a success.

Most of these costs can be obtained from your staff or from companies who can provide you the components you require in your community site. For most justifications, a one year budget is sufficient to show the effectiveness of the plan and its ability to recover the initial investment costs. If your situation is different, the budget process and effectiveness measures are the same but are calculated over a number of years.

The next graphic is a sample budget. Notice the budget is organized in simple-to-view areas showing the year-one investments of the organization. These summary numbers are supported by detailed spreadsheets the marketing team can reference to answer questions from senior management.

For some of the costs, calculation details are given. You can see them in the marketing costs. Other budgets don't show them at all. They key is to have them for questions or when a more detailed discussion is needed.

	Category	Cost
	Development	
Community Website		$150,000
Mobile App		$400,000
Database Management		$15,000
	Operation	
Web and Mobile		$180,000
*Maintanence Fee: 15,000/month		
Employee		$186,000
*Employee Salary: $62,000/yr * 3		
	Marketing	
Facebook		$18,250
*Facebook Advertising Cost: $50/day		
Twitter		$10,950
*Twitter Advertising Cost: $30/day		
YouTube		$200,000
*$0.10-$0.30 (cost per view)		
Banner Ads		$50,000
*$15-$85CPM (cost per 1k impressions)		
City Guides/Online Brochures		$36,000
*$3000/month		
Blogger Endorsement (PPC based		$45,000
*$1.5/click		
Online Community		$40,000
Email		$900
*reach 5001-10,000 people $75/mon		
Total Marketing Cost		$401,100
Total Cost		$1,332,100

While your one year budget may make sense and be a small investment against the revenue potential of the target market (in this case it was 23 million people at $180 average purchase price), management may not want to immediately make the total investment. To facilitate this type of discussion, we recommend creating a pilot program budget.

The pilot program is a partial program which might run three to six months. To create it, you take the one year budget and strip it down to the essential elements by getting rid of the nice to haves. Generally, you keep most of the Go Viral marketing plan, the database and key pages within the site, and the empowering or awesome type of content. Also keep most of the marketing and IT support.

What you eliminate are some of the components included to keep people coming back to the community. While this might seem counterintuitive, it isn't when you consider the role of the pilot project.

Because senior management might be skeptical of the entire program, a pilot program is designed to show them it will work and achieve their growth and revenue goals. The pilot project is not designed to exist forever by itself. It's designed as a fast test of the concept over a short period of time. When the pilot program hits the initial steps in the relationship funnel, and proves the plan will bring the right target market, at quantity, to the private virtual community site, the pilot proves its effectiveness. It is not a stand-alone plan but a stripped down version to prove concept and approve the larger expenditure. For the example shown, the pilot plan budget for a three month program was $255,750.

Step 3: Develop "What-If" Metrics to Determine Success

For many of the steps in your relationship funnel, you don't have the experience to know exactly how many will move to each level and continue the process toward becoming customers. For most companies, the unknown steps start with the number who will find the landing page. While you know the total market and the total number who are in the social sphere, the rest is an unknown—and senior management doesn't like unknowns. To alleviate their fears and also generate key metrics for your justification, you need to fill in the unknown steps. To accomplish this, you will need to perform a series of "What If" analyses.

A "What If" analysis is one in which you use your marketing and business knowledge to create three possible scenarios for each unknown step in the relationship funnel. Develop an optimistic, average or neutral, and a pessimistic assumption about possible performance. These percentages and numbers are not created in a vacuum but are based on your analysis of each step and the metrics most likely to be generated.

Optimistic Estimation				
Market	**Rate**	**Volume**	**Revenue**	**Total**
TOTAL		33,700,000		
Social	50%	16,850,000		
Landing	10%	1,685,000		
Registration	30%	505,500		
Product Evaluati(	20%	101,100		
First Purchase	10%	10,110	$180	$1,819,800
Repeat Purchase	2%	202	$180	$36,396
Total				$1,856,196
ROI				306%

Neutral Estimation				
Market	**Rate**	**Volume**	**Revenue**	**Total**
TOTAL		33,700,000		
Social	50%	16,850,000		
Landing	10%	1,685,000		
Registration	30%	505,500		
Product Evaluati(	20%	101,100		
First Purchase	5%	5,055	$180	$909,900
Repeat Purchase	2%	101	$180	$18,198
Total				$928,098
ROI				153%

Pessimistic Estimation / Break Even				
Market	**Rate**	**Volume**	**Revenue**	**Total**
TOTAL		33,700,000		
Social	50%	16,850,000		
Landing	10%	1,685,000		
Registration	25%	421,250		
Product Evaluation	16%	66,558		
First Purchase	5%	3,328	$180	$599,018
Repeat Purchase	1%	33	$180	$5,990
Total				$605,008
ROI				100%

From this example, you'll note the total and the social quantities are identical. This example is for a very nonsocial market, so the team identified that only 50 percent would be a social target for this very niche program. After those two steps, they presented three different relationship funnels with three different sets of assumptions for each subsequent step.

Note in the example, registration—the number of prospects who will reach the landing page and register over the course of a year is 30 percent in the top two scenarios, and 25 percent in the pessimistic. This percentage and number represent the number of prospects who will move from the social cloud and be motivated to become a part of this organization's virtual private community. To generate these numbers is the responsibility of the Go Viral marketing program and investment. This means your aggregate marketing program must generate at least 25 percent of the total market in the year.

Before you become concerned about this particular funnel's performance, let me state that this is an extremely niched trigger event market where the prospects are actively seeking information and tools to address their personal challenges—exactly what this organization's empowering concept will provide. For most companies, your Go Viral type marketing program will likely only produce 1 percent or even less of the target market for your initial investment. Don't be too concerned about the metrics. Just look at the results.

As you go down the marketing funnels, you can see the numbers and resulting percentages the team is anticipating for their program. The key is you want to show the efficiency of the program from top to bottom and the final customer counts and revenues you'll likely see if you implement the program. The performance level between each step shows the effectiveness of your marketing program, landing pages and other components that impact prospect performance. It gives you some initial performance expectations you can use to both sell the program to senior management and to manage the program over time.

In this example, note the number of prospects hitting the landing page and completing the registration process is extremely low. This means most of the individuals who start the registration process will not complete it. While the metrics work for this example, your marketing managers will want to focus on developing a plan to improve these low numbers. From the economics, a small improvement in registration completions will produce more solid bottom-line results.

If you examine the steps before and after registration, there are two possible reasons for the low registration rate. Before registration, if your Go Viral marketing program is attracting people who really don't belong to the community, they will not register. You might want to tighten your target to improve results. Another potential reason is your landing page or registration page asks too many questions or doesn't sell the empowering concept. You may want to test alternate pages to see if you can improve results.

What this shows is the importance of understanding the relationship funnel and its actual uses within your marketing effort. Ideally, you want a relationship funnel with strong response and activity rates from top to bottom. When that doesn't happen, you need to test different approaches to improve your results. When you have an efficient relationship funnel, your marketing program will be effective in acquiring and building strong relationships with your high-value target market(s).

Step 4: Calculate Your Success Metrics to Justify Your Program

This final step is where the relationship funnel really helps sell the program. For senior management, there are two key calculations you need to develop to really sell your social marketing plan. The first is break even, and the second is return on investment. With these two calculations, your budgets, your relationship funnel and your plan details, you have the information you need to present the plan and its benefits.

When presented with a new marketing plan, the first question senior managers want to know is, "What is our risk with this plan?" The break-even attempts to quantify this risk. In developing any of your social strategies, you start by quantifying the total market and using this market size as the start of your relationship funnel. In addition, you also examined the target market and established an average first purchase revenue amount. Your goal is to get a small part of the total market to make that first purchase. You then proceed to build the program and establish the budget. As a result of this work, you now have the basic information you need to create your break-even numbers.

The break-even calculation is designed to show the minimum number of purchases you need to recover the costs of the marketing investment. To calculate it, you need to divide the total budget dollars by the average first purchase revenue. This yields a count of the number of product sales you need to make to cover the cost of the program. It is your absolute minimum number of sales. It is not a goal.

To simply present this number to senior management minimizes its impact. Ideally, you want to show them that, compared to the size of the total market, the number needed to break-even is extremely low. In other words, you don't need to move much of the total target market to pay for your program. This makes the risk somewhat lower.

Number of Gen X moms using social media	14,000,000
Goal for the number of online registrations	200,000
Market penetration	1.43%
Annual revenue per new customer	$2,286.00
No. of new customers needed to break-even	712
Break-even Conversion rate	0.35%

Take a look at this break-even calculation from a different client. They are targeting Gen X moms and found 14 million in the target market. Their Social IMC plan would likely yield 200,000 registrants. This is a penetration into the target market of 1.43 percent.

For the product they're selling, the average first purchase revenue is $2,246. Dividing 712 by 200,000 means they need to sell about a third of 1 percent (.35 percent) of their anticipated registration group to recover the costs of the marketing program. This shows they need to move a relatively small part of their private virtual community to action to recover their marketing investment.

They could also have divided 712 by 14 million to show the extremely small percentage of the total market they need to move to customer status to recover their marketing investment. In most cases, you'll find your social strategy, while having a relatively large budget, will require only a minimum number of sales within the large target market to recover your marketing budget. Break-even helps to put this into perspective and make it a less risky sale to senior management.

The final calculation is Return on Investment (ROI) or ROMI (Return on Marketing Investment). The difference between these is ROMI does not need to have a full financial analysis to take into consideration all cost factors within the organization. Instead, it looks at the return on investment the marketing dollars will yield given the three "What If" assumptions. ROMI is easier for marketers to calculate and manage as they're focused on deploying marketing programs designed to return more dollars to the organization. How those dollars are used internally across the organization is something they cannot control or manage. Therefore, ROMI is an effective metric for senior management and one that can be used by the CMO and their team to manage the program over time.

Return on Marketing Investment (ROMI)

Goal for the number of online registrations	200,000
Goal for the number of new customers	1,200
Conversion rate	0.60%
Annual revenue per new customer	$2,286.00
Estimated revenue	$2,743,200.00
Total Budget	$1,689,600.00
Estimated Incremental Contribution Margin	$1,053,600.00
ROMI	**162.36%**

From the same case study, the likely goal of the program was 200,000 people. Given the likely conversion rate of .60 percent, this yields 1,200 new customers. (Remember, the break-even was 712). These 1,200 new customers would purchase $2.7 million in revenues against a first year investment budget of $1.689 million. This contributed $1.05 million to the organization's bottom line.

If you divide the estimated revenue by the total budget, you get an ROMI of 162 percent. This means every dollar you invest returns $1.62 in revenue (within the first year). This calculation tells senior management this is a good investment for the organization. It also tells them that even if the marketing assumptions are off a bit, there is room in the plan to at least break even. This minimizes their risk when they accept your marketing plan.

Because two of the three strategies link the social strategy to bottom-line measures, this lets your marketing team manage their social activities in the same fashion as all their other marketing channels. Each program has a relationship funnel with key metrics for every step, an established budget to drive the program forward and key senior management metrics the CMO and their team can manage over the history of the program. It makes your social investment simply another part of your total marketing plan while still retaining the unique characteristics social brings to your organization. By linking social to the bottom-line sales systems of your organization, you make it a trackable and measurable system using the metrics senior management needs to make their budget decisions.

10

Which Strategy is Best for Your Organization?

So it all comes down to this one question. Which strategy is best for you? The answer may surprise you. You really need all three. But, you need to consider using them for the different markets you want to develop.

Engagement marketing is ideal for certain situations. While it lacks the ability to have a two-way, database driven connection with the target market, engagement marketing works well for your lower value markets and for the distribution of general content. It's great for making new product announcements. If you do something fun and really awesome, it can easily go viral within your target market.

Engagement marketing is also useful if you want to distribute coupons or announce special sales. It is also useful for general product or organization announcements. You can communicate with your broad target markets through the social networking sites as well as in appropriate virtual communities. It's a great way to get your message through to your broadest audience in a cost effective manner.

Nurture Marketing is a preferred strategy for the high-value markets you need to nurture to move them from prospect to customer. Its ability to make a relevant connection based on their interests and needs and then move them forward in a tailored nurturing system makes Nurture Marketing a preferred strategy for many sales and marketing organizations. It creates a database, determines an individual's persona and their point in the product purchase decision process, and then moves them, systematically, toward a sale. It is very effective and used by companies ranging from start-ups to the Fortune 100.

Finally, Social IMC is an ideal strategy for your highest-value markets. Done effectively, this strategy moves these high-value individuals off the grid to your virtual community offering. As you continue to meet their needs, a special bond forms between them and your organization—a bond that is strong when it comes time to buy.

With Social IMC, you are able to best position your organization and your brands, engage in a knowledge-based interaction with community members, and deeply understand their needs, wants, and desires. While it takes a larger investment and dedicated individuals to maintain and grow the community, for most companies it is well worth the effort. By sheltering and building the strongest possible relationship with your highest value markets, you place your organization in a strong position to maintain and, in most cases, grow your market share in these valuable markets.

Engagement Marketing	Nurture Marketing	Social IMC
Target Broadly	Target Interests	Target Communities
Create Awesome	Create Relevant	Create Empowerment
Go Social	"Go Fishing"	Go Viral
Entertain	Classify	Identify
Strengthen	Nurture	Engage

The key to social marketing success is to match the strategy with the potential value of your target market. Like all forms of integrated marketing, the key is to start with the market and its relative value to your organization. Based on its size and potential value, you select the strategy most appropriate for each market. Once the strategy is established, you then build the program to reach the target markets using the media channels they most prefer, including social channels. You then engage and—in most strategies—acquire them as prospects and customers. Your challenge is to then move them through their product purchase lifecycle toward first purchase. Essentially, the market dictates your strategy, the level of investment, and the type of acquisition program you need to sustain the social strategy. As with all forms of integrated marketing, the market drives the strategy, not the other way around.

Mix and Match

One important point for business-to-business organizations: you may want to vary your social strategies by the various target markets you have within the organization. Generally in business-to-business marketing, major purchases are made by a team of individuals from the organization. These are the decision makers who are generally the senior management of the organization, influencers, specialists who will manage the product when it's used within the organization, and the users—people who will actually use it. From a social perspective, you should consider using Social IMC to engage and influence the decision makers.

One client uses a private virtual website and webinars with key business leaders to engage the CEOs, CFOs, and CMOs who will eventually make the purchase decisions for the organization. For the purchase managers, engineers, and other user groups, they deploy a Nurture Marketing program. This program provides relevant e-books and white papers to engage with these influencer and user groups.

They then database them, determine where they're at in the product purchase lifecycle, and then send them relevant new content to move them toward an eventual product purchase. For the other segments within their target companies, the organization has social networking sites on Facebook and LinkedIn, and uses Twitter to provide general content, new organization announcements, and other content designed for a more general market.

Mixing and matching your social strategies allows you to tailor your message and your relationship to each target market. It develops them in the most effective way and builds the type of relationships that is most likely to result in a purchase. Keep in mind each target market is different and you need to determine the best social strategy to build the right relationship—especially for your high-value markets.

While these three strategies are the base for social marketing today, they are continually evolving. I will keep these strategies updated on my Social IMC website at (www.SocialIMC.com). Feel free to link up, make comments, and watch new videos and case studies for companies that are continually improving and advancing each of these strategies. In my graduate course, I find the syllabus remains relevant for only about half a year. It then needs to be rewritten to encompass new technologies and new sites impacting our business and consumer markets. So, too, with this book. I look forward to meeting you on Social IMC and hope you enjoyed examining these three social strategies.

Endnotes

1 http://dstevenwhite.com/2013/02/09/social-media-growth-2006-to-2012/

2 http://0312f31.netsolhost.com/WordPress/wp-content/uploads/2013/04/Pew-SocNet-Site-Use-by-Age-Feb2013.png

3 http://trends.e-strategyblog.com/wp-content/uploads/2012/12/socialnetworkusergrowth.gif

4 http://www-01.ibm.com/common/ssi/cgi-bin/ssialias?subtype=XB&infotype=PM&appname=GBSE_GB_TI_USEN&htmlfid=GBE03419USEN&attachment=GBE03419USEN.PDF

5 http://www.marketingsherpa.com/resources/MS-2011-Social-Marketing-Benchmark-Report-EXCERPT.pdf

6 http://news.cnet.com/8301-1023_3-57601796-93/facebooks-biggest-challenge-too-many-people-like-it/

7 http://www.theguardian.com/technology/2013/nov/10/teenagers-messenger-apps-facebook-exodus

8 http://www-935.ibm.com/services/us/en/c-suite/ceostudy2012/#

9 http://www.jeffbullas.com/2012/05/23/35-mind-numbing-youtube-facts-figures-and-statistics-infographic/

10 http://socialmediatoday.com/socialbarrel/1650226/second-largest-search-engine-infographic

11 http://www.tenouk.com/learningretentionrate.html

12 http://socialmediatoday.com/mikevelocity/1698201/blogging-stats-2013-infographic

13 http://www.bruceclay.com/blog/2012/02/virtual-world-versus-physical-world/

14 http://www.justjared.com/2011/07/29/heidi-klum-one-day-youre-in-and-one-day-youre-out/

15 http://www.gamification.org/

16 http://www.upworthy.com/could-this-be-the-most-upworthy-site-in-the-history-of-the-internet

17 http://www.jeffbullas.com/2013/02/11/the-facts-and-figures-on-youtube-in-2013-infographic/

18 http://youtu.be/fD1WqPGn5Ag

19 http://youtu.be/fD1WqPGn5Ag

20 http://youtu.be/uHtDRw4ujYw

21 http://econsultancy.com/us/blog/10370-cadbury-s-shift-to-social-means-no-more-drumming-gorillas

22 http://econsultancy.com/us/blog/10370-cadbury-s-shift-to-social-means-no-more-drumming-gorillas

23 http://econsultancy.com/us/blog/10370-cadbury-s-shift-to-social-means-no-more-drumming-gorillas

24 http://www.digitalbuzzblog.com/wp-content/uploads/2012/01/Cadbury-Infographic.jpg

25 http://www.netprospex.com/SmarterData.aspx

26 http://www.SilverPop.com/About/About-SilverPop/

27 http://www.youtube.com/watch?v=DBNf4CeATxg&feature=share&list=PL6LFs_QnWsyulZMsKoIaUrKhYb5q1QFDn

28 http://www.rollingstone.com/music/videos/mumford-sons-elvis-costello-cover-the-ghost-of-tom-joad-for-agit8-20130611

29 http://www.ogilvy.co.za/2011/11/carling-black-label-be-the-coach-case-study/